# Treasures in Heaven

**Treasures in Heaven**

Huldah Buntain
as told to
B. W. Corpany
and Hal Donaldson

Copyright © 1989 by Calcutta Mission of Mercy
Printed in the United States of America
ISBN: 0-88368-217-6

*Cover photography and design by Terry Dugan.*

Unless otherwise noted, Scripture quotations are taken from the
*New King James Version.* Copyright © 1979, 1980, 1982, Thomas
Nelson Inc., Publishers. Scripture quotations marked *KJV* are taken
from the *King James Version* of the Bible.

# *Dedication*

In loving memory of Mark Buntain.

# *Acknowledgement*

Special thanks to the Bethesda Foundation and the Calcutta Mission of Mercy for making this book possible.

My deepest appreciation goes to Jim and Bonnie Long, Alice Southard, Carol Corpany, Dan Scherling, Lionel Maddaford, Scott Craven, Vern Kingsland, Lisa Rich, Judi Schultz, Steve Donaldson, David Donaldson, and my caring wife, Doree.

I am also indebted to Mark and Huldah Buntain. In the course of my journalistic pursuits I have interviewed politicians, millionaires, professional athletes, and Hollywood celebrities. None, however, has left such an indelible impression on my life as these two missionaries. My concept of successful Christian living has been uprooted—not by listening to their words or calculating their monumental accomplishments, but by watching them walk through the crowded back alleys of Calcutta and sensing their genuine love for their fellow man. They preached to me through their deeds and gave the gospel new meaning.

Thank you. I'll never be the same.

Hal Donaldson

# *Authors' Note*

Many of the descriptions of India are accounts made prior to the present government's rise to power. India has made great strides in recent years.

This is a true story. At the authors' discretion, some incidents have been altered in the interest of dramatic continuity.

# *Foreword*

I first met Huldah Buntain in May, 1980. We were at the Vance Hotel near the Seattle-Tacoma airport where the Calcutta Mission of Mercy Board of Directors was meeting. I was being interviewed for my present position as Executive Director of CMM. I soon recognized that Huldah was a very busy person with vast responsibilities.

Over the past nine years, I have developed an even greater appreciation for her and her ability to efficiently accomplish a myriad of tasks. Every time I journey to Calcutta, I marvel at her workload and stamina. I have seen her, after a long, difficult work week, spend her Sunday afternoon writing letters to donors or visiting the sick.

To me and many others who know her well, Huldah Buntain is the "miracle of Calcutta." Thirty-five years ago, she was reluctant to go to India. The mere idea of taking her small baby to a foreign country was, to say the least, unthinkable. But Huldah set aside her fears and traveled halfway around the world so she and her husband, Mark, could expose thousands to the love of Jesus Christ.

*Treasures in Heaven* unveils many of the hardships and trials she encountered during her lifetime. More importantly, it reveals how she triumphed. Her story is a gripping portrait of one woman's courage and a God who gave comfort in times of distress.

Through all the challenges, Huldah remained committed to the Lord, her husband, and the people of Calcutta.

I was reminded of her unyielding loyalty to Mark on one occasion in particular. Just before we were to leave for the airport to see Huldah off to Calcutta, our staff workers were standing with her in the reception area of our Calcutta Mission of Mercy office.

"Huldah," I asked before leading the group in prayer, "why don't you just stay here and work out of this office for a while so you can be closer to your children, grandchildren, and friends?"

Without hesitation, she said, "I have to go back. My husband is there."

What has impressed me the most about Huldah is her unassuming style. She has never chased notoriety.

I was standing near her when Mark received an honorary doctorate from the University of Missouri, Columbia. After the honor was bestowed, I whispered to Huldah, "You deserve half of that doctorate."

She turned and said politely, "Thank you, but I don't need any recognition."

I believed her, for that is the kind of person she is—one who is mounting up *treasures in heaven*.

B. W. Corpany

# Contents

# 1

# *Is This Heaven?*

"Now boarding through gate 54, Thai Airlines flight 731, from Seattle to Tokyo and Bangkok."

Instantly, anxious passengers collected their carry-ons and headed toward the gate. I lagged behind, absorbing each tick of the clock, dreading the lonely marathon flight back to Calcutta—my home for more than thirty years.

My sister-in-law, Alice, gave me a farewell embrace, and within moments I found myself walking down the gangplank to the jetliner.

Moisture—not enough to form a tear—accumulated in my eyes as I pondered leaving America and my loved ones behind. I had made this departure many times over the years, but it had never become easy.

Waiting for me in Calcutta would be my missionary husband, Mark Buntain, and a city teeming with millions of impoverished, diseased people. Having just spent four weeks in the States, my sympathetic, grieving emotions had been given a much needed recess.

The layover in Bangkok and the one-hour stopover in Tokyo were blessings in disguise—opportunities to prepare myself for the adjustment I would endure upon arriving back in Calcutta. Although I had witnessed the human plight there countless times before, I could never grow accustomed to the awful stench of this teeming city and the sight of malnourished children.

As I deboarded the airliner at dusk in magnificent Tokyo, again I was reminded that this brilliant city, so different from Calcutta, was my birthplace. But Tokyo had changed. Exquisitely designed skyscrapers had replaced the time-worn British structures built a century ago. And the Japanese, bustling by on the crowded streets, now wore jeans and business suits instead of their native dress.

Some things, however, had remained the same. The familiar scented sea breeze sweeping off the Bay of Tokyo brushed my face and brought with it fond memories of my missionary childhood and my godly mother and father.

My parents, Reverend Alex and Gwendolyn Munroe, had made their initial voyage to Japan in 1918. My grandmother, who was suffering with a stomach ulcer, at first opposed the missionary journey, not wanting to be distanced from her only daughter. But after much debate she finally granted her blessing. My parents worked in Tokyo for several years before taking a furlough to Canada. During this furlough, my older sister Beulah was born.

Upon returning to Tokyo for a second term, my family found the city had been devastated by an earthquake. As their ship was docking, my parents saw that the once majestic city now more closely resembled a rock quarry, with brick and concrete structures relegated to piles of rubble. With nowhere to retreat, they had to remain on board for several days and then slept in a large crate used to ship the family automobile.

I was born in Tokyo in 1926 and grew up amidst a congregation of Japanese converts who had accepted Jesus Christ as Savior at my father's evangelistic center—the first church of its kind in Tokyo. The center was started by a small group of believers who met in an abandoned pencil factory built against the towering wall of a prison facility.

Before every service, like a drum major, Dad led a small band of musical instruments in a march down a main street, inviting listeners to join the parade and follow them to church. Dad, who was an exceptional speaker, preached every sermon as if it were meant for the ears of high-ranking nobility. The center was usually packed, with people from all walks of life singing and worshiping together. I can still hear the sweet, melodious sounds as they respectfully praised God as one voice in their native language.

Besides ministering to their own church, my parents also exerted a spiritual influence on the other missionaries. Actually, God used Beulah to spur the missionaries to reassess their doctrinal positions on healing. She had suffered with infantile paralysis. My parents carried her everywhere, and with each cumbersome step they prayed that she would be healed. The other missionaries thought my parents' decision not to send Beulah to the States to receive proper treatment bordered on cruelty. They neither believed nor taught divine healing.

But one summer, while all the missionaries were together vacationing in the foothills, God chose to heal Beulah. To their amazement, my sister stood to her feet for the first time in answer to my parents' persistent prayers. As a result of her healing, the missionaries and many churches in Tokyo experienced a spiritual reawakening. Dad always said her healing had been delayed so the other missionaries would believe in the restoration power of the Almighty.

One of my most vivid memories of my childhood in Tokyo dates back to the early 1930s. Although a very small child at the time, I remember being awakened by a terrifying eruption of voices and sirens. Ordinarily, Tokyo slumbered before dawn, with the demanding sounds of railtrains, taxis, rickshaws, and the voices of pedestrians not yet ringing from the business district. But this particular night, the city had been instantly brought to life by an onslaught of nature: an earthquake. For all I knew the entire planet was shaking apart at its foundations.

Outside our window, two kerosene lamps that were suspended from wooden posts first oscillated like pendulums and then shattered as they collided with the earth. Then the posts themselves danced out of the ground. Quivering bushes shed their leaves. Cabinets and tables capsized as wall hangings sailed through the air.

Beulah and I screamed hysterically as our beds tossed us from one side to the other like cowboys riding wild broncos. Before we could be thrown from our saddles, my father rescued us—one in each arm—and deposited us safely on the front lawn.

I watched with amazement as some of the simple bamboo houses around us tumbled apart like matchbook houses. The thick stalk supports on front porches snapped like pencils, and the foundations crumbled like pie crust.

At that moment Dad discovered that Mother had been trapped inside. "Jesus, help us!" he cried. My heart stood still as we watched Dad bravely inch his way over a crumbled wall and back into the unsteady house. The stairway to the second floor had collapsed, and Mother was standing on what was now an unsupported catwalk. A cloud of dust blanketed her flannel robe. The room shook again. Bamboo rods fell from the bedroom ceiling as if the house were under a fierce air attack.

Somehow, moments later, they staggered through a portal filled with debris. Relief flooded my tiny soul. Clinging to one another, we watched helplessly, wondering if ours, like the other homes around us, would dissipate into a smoldering heap.

Fortunately, once the trembling and destruction came to a halt, the parsonage was still standing. After surveying the structural damage, we realized we couldn't live there.

We moved our salvageable belongings into the church my father pastored. There, the wooden pews became our beds. Dad did his best to convince us that living at the church was a privilege despite its minor inconveniences. I soon discovered he was right as I amused myself by crawling under pews, banging the keys of the church's upright piano, and "playing church."

When I played church—usually with the pews empty—I had to preach, play the piano, lead songs, and take up an offering all by myself. Occasionally, I convinced Beulah to participate, but usually I was the entire show.

My parents never discouraged my charades. In fact, they sometimes participated. Dad occasionally plopped a yen or two in the offering plate as I shoved it under his nose, and when Mother wasn't busy, she gladly sat in a pew and made believe she was listening to my sermonettes. I was too small to stand behind the pulpit, but sometimes I glanced at mother from the platform and saw her trying to conceal her sniggering, her lips slightly parted in a smile.

I can't remember *what* I preached, but I remember mimicking Dad by waving my arms in the air. Mother often yelled "amen" whenever I said something that made sense, and nothing in those few instances could have made me happier. My parents' encouragement made me feel like a genuine preacher.

Shortly after the earthquake that damaged our house, my parents made plans to return to Canada. Mother's severe migraine headaches had made it impossible for her to withstand Tokyo's intense heat, and my father felt God was leading us home.

I distinctly remember our oceanliner docking in Victoria, British Columbia, after the long journey from Japan. For all of my early years, I had heard wonderful stories about life in "B.C." But I was most anxious to meet this woman Beulah called "Grandma."

I was yo-yo-ing up and down on the deck, asking in Japanese, "Where is she, Mommy?"

"I don't see her yet," Mother said.

My heels were clicking with impatience. "What does she look like?"

"She'll probably be wearing a hat. She likes hats." Suddenly she pointed to a woman wearing a pink hat in the crowd below. "There she is."

My eyes searched but could not locate her. I tugged on Mother's dress. "Where?"

I spotted her before Mother could respond.

I began racing around the deck, pointing and screaming to the passengers in Japanese and English that the woman in the small rimmed hat was my grandmother. Most of the Caucasian passengers couldn't understand me. Even so, Mother didn't let me stray too far and collared me back to the railing amidst a crowd of chuckling travelers.

Once we deboarded, out from behind a young, embracing couple emerged my grandmother. She pushed toward Mother and Dad with her arms outstretched. Mother's brother, Uncle Lionel, was a few strides behind her. Uncle Lionel hugged Beulah and me simultaneously by pressing us to his hips. Then Grandma gave us each a hug, my feet nearly lifting from the ground as she drew me to her breast. Then she stepped back for an extensive, peculiar look at her two granddaughters.

She smiled. "I think they have your coloring, Gwendolyn," she said, "and Huldah looks like you, Alex. Wait until your Grandpa gets a look at you two."

Grandma kept staring at us, almost as if she were looking for a trace of herself in our faces. I didn't mind, though. I was enjoying the extra attention. My hands latched onto her arm, and I remember the sense of love and security that enveloped me.

As we threaded our way toward the car, I tried to look everywhere at once. I had never seen *so* blue a sky and *so* bright a sun. Everything seemed clean and new. I asked my mother, "Is this place heaven?"

"No, this isn't heaven," she answered.

I knew she was right, but at that moment an inner awareness of the beauty and serenity of our future, eternal home was fixed in my heart—a memory I would often return to in the years ahead.

# 2
## *"Please Don't Go"*

My grandparents, Francis and Isobel Maddaford, first came to Canada from England when Mother was a young girl. Grandpa was a five-foot-eight-inch policeman who became a preacher shortly after accepting Christ as his Savior. Together they founded Glad Tidings Rescue Mission in downtown Vancouver, British Columbia.

The brick mission building appeared innocuous enough, but on Sundays few places were more popular in downtown Vancouver. Grandpa's mission attracted more down-and-outers than the other welfare and food distribution lines that seemed to stretch every block in the downtown area.

These were the bleak days of the Depression, and my grandfather's preaching and compassion for the poor attracted a large group, mostly gray bearded men with nothing more to do with their hands than clutch onto nearly empty bottles of whiskey and beg for dimes. Because he didn't allow alcohol inside the mission, Grandpa conveniently placed a garbage can outside the door for the disposing of liquor. Many of the men willingly discarded their bottles just to find shelter from the cold and place their hands next to the mission's old boiler heater.

We lived with my grandparents in Vancouver for a short time until Dad established a church on Broad Street in nearby Victoria.

Despite interspersing more English phrases with my Japanese, I couldn't converse with my grandparents very well. It was easy, however, to sense their affection. Their hugs and smiles said more than words ever could.

One evening, while my parents were away, I began pleading with Grandma to give me some water to drink.

"Mesu," I called from my bed.

Grandma looked at me in bewilderment.

"Mesu, Mesu," I repeated.

She offered me a blanket, then a toy, then a pillow. After she had tried everything within reach to satisfy my request, she finally threw up her hands. She was relieved when my parents walked through the door and promptly handed me a cup of water and put an end to my pleading.

Grandma loved to brush her fingers through my thick locks of hair and tickle my stomach. Grandpa was just as affectionate and caring. With lines butterflying from his eyes and the dark brown bleached from his hair, Grandpa appeared much older than Grandma. Even his voice did not resound with the force of a typical preacher. Nevertheless, I will always remember his unwavering compassion for the poor and homeless. For many of the transients who frequented Grandpa's mission, he was the closest person they had to a father. His cheery disposition and loving ways gave many unfortunate men reason to awake from their stupors. Even the intoxicated lushes who ordinarily had difficulty saying their own names could not ignore his pleas for salvation.

I loved tagging along with Grandpa and following him around the mission. He never seemed to mind. I think I served as a radiant symbol, a reminder that the world was more than just winos and derelicts.

"Why do these men come here?" I asked one afternoon, hopping up on his desk.

"They need help."

I had so many questions pent up inside me. I was always known as the "question box" of the family. "Do they pay, Grandpa?"

"No, they don't have any money."

"Oh," I moaned with disappointment. "Who buys the food then?"

"God gives us all the food and money we need."

"Oh," I acknowledged, my frown disappearing. "How does God know what kind of food to send?"

Grandpa began laughing so hard that Mother rushed in to see what had sent him into convulsions.

Some months later, my parents were summoned from our Victoria home to Grandpa's room. He had suddenly taken ill. Although they wouldn't let us into his room that night, the odor drifting from the bedroom reminded me of the disinfectant Mother dabbed on our scraped knees from time to time. A balding doctor arrived moments later and immediately rushed in to tend to Grandpa. Beulah and I waited patiently outside the bedroom door that shielded us from the unfolding drama. That night was the beginning of Grandpa's decline.

In the weeks that followed, Beulah and I saw very little of Grandpa's fatigued, shrinking face. He was obviously growing weaker and unable to muster smiles as frequently as he once had. The doctor had diagnosed his condition as stomach cancer.

Then the dreaded call came from Mother—who had been staying with Grandpa during his illness—instructing Dad to bring Beulah and me to his room, for he was not expected to live.

Dad was unusually quiet, almost solemn as he drove us to Grandpa's house.

Beulah and I once again took our places outside Grandpa's room, like two grammar school students awaiting orders to enter a principal's office. I was afraid, for I had seen Mother leave the room crying, teetering, with Dad supporting her shivering arms.

Finally Dad escorted us into Grandpa's chamber. The blankets were pulled up to his chin. I couldn't believe that Grandpa was inside the ashen face that glared at me. Tears began to blur my vision as if the room were being overtaken by an eerie fog. The gray walls seemed to be creeping in on Grandpa's bed. It suddenly occurred to me that his life was culminating, and nobody could do anything about it.

His wrinkled fist unraveled and reached for our hands. Reluctantly, I guided my palm toward his. My fingers could feel the faintest pulse. He first talked and prayed with Beulah and then in a struggled whisper, said, "Huldah."

I didn't know what to say.

"Huldah," he gasped again.

"She's here, Grandpa," my father confirmed. "Answer him, Huldah."

"Hul . . . dah?" Grandpa phrased in the form of a question.

My lips quivered as I answered. "Yes, Grandpa. I'm here."

"I love you, Huldah."

"Grandpa, don't leave," I begged, tears still flowing.

"God is calling me home, child."

"No," I defied. "Please don't go."

Dad whispered into my ear, "Just tell him how much you love him."

"Huldah, close your eyes," Grandpa requested softly.

Dad nodded for me to obey.

"Dear God," Grandpa prayed. "I know You love Huldah very much and have a great work for her to do. Help her, dear heavenly Father, to understand why You have chosen to take me home."

I opened my eyes as he took a deep breath and coughed. He seemed to collect his strength, then continued. "Help her to carry on the tradition of ministry You have given our family and give her a special anointing."

All of a sudden his prayer ended. I reopened my eyes to be sure the inevitable hadn't happened. His thin-veined eyelids were closed, but he was still breathing.

"I love you, Grandpa," I stammered as I wrapped my hands around his dangling arm. "I love you."

He had exhausted his words. With his last surge of energy, he reached his right hand across his body to pat me on the head. I knew then that not even death could devalue our friendship. Even though he was going far away, I was certain he would never forget me.

I would never see him again. The next day I was told he had died.

# 3
# *Hard Times*

Grandfather's death did something more to me than bathe my face in tears; it compelled me at a young age to consider the frailty and brevity of human existence. Furthermore, I guess it was the first time, as a grammar-schooler, that I seriously asked myself if there truly was a heaven and a hell.

Memories of Grandpa's funeral swirled through my mind in the days and weeks that followed. During the ceremony, Mother had to stay by Grandma's side, so her second cousin, Mrs. Annie Hammond—who we called "Auntie Annie"—was handed the chore of watching Beulah and me.

The platform and casket were in full view. As Dad strode to the pulpit to conduct the ceremony before a capacity crowd, I looked up at Auntie Annie and asked, "Why did Grandpa have to die?"

She said, "Honey, that's something only God knows. But at least he's with God in heaven."

"I know," I whimpered.

Auntie Annie soothingly cradled my head in her arms and said, "Someday you'll see your grandfather again in heaven. Just think about that."

In time, after deciding for myself that there must be a heaven, Grandpa's death became easier to accept. I remember talking to him one night, hoping he was listening from the clouds: "If you hear me, Grandpa, I hope you're having a lot of fun . . . whatever you're doing. I miss you so much. So does everyone else. Dad is going to take over the mission, so don't worry," I said, trying to think of other news that might interest him. "Well, I better go to sleep now. I love you, Grandpa."

After Grandpa died, Uncle Lionel took care of my grandmother, who was still suffering with a stomach disorder. Uncle Lionel was a polite, distinguished businessman who enjoyed golfing and playing the piano. He never married, presuming it unfair to bring a wife into his home when his sickly mother needed his care. He occasionally gave Beulah and me gifts and nicknamed us, affectionately, "Bubbles and Squeaks."

Grandmother's ill health made it nearly impossible for her to help at the mission, so Dad agreed to leave his pastorate and assume leadership of the outreach. Dad soon turned the facility into an evangelistic center that continued to meet the needs of the poor while functioning as a church.

One afternoon two men came to Dad claiming they were unemployed and begging for one of his revered food vouchers. This slip of paper entitled them to a meal at a downtown cafeteria called the White Lunch; the cost of the meal would then be charged to the church. But when Dad received the bill for their dinners, *twenty* meals had been charged to his account. An entire regiment of freeloaders had eaten at the church's expense. At first Dad was visibly upset; then he realized he was at fault for failing to record the number of meals he was approving on the voucher slip.

The 1930s were difficult for North Americans; many went without food and proper shelter. The food lines often became battle zones, with protests and riots breaking out.

On one occasion, vagrants threw bottles through the window of Woodward's department store, which was adjacent to the church. Fortunately, the police arrived to put an end to the fracas before the men damaged the mission front. Dad, nonetheless, warned us to be careful.

Although we always had food on the table and shoes on our feet, our family experienced its share of financial hardship. One Christmas in particular, Beulah and I had to share a gift.

"Beulah, Huldah," Dad said with a glum look on his face, "we were only able to buy you two gifts this year. I think you're going to like them. They are nice gifts, but you're going to have to share them."

Since there were only two gifts under the Christmas tree, we had already come to that unpleasant conclusion. We knew our parents loved us and did what they could to make the holiday memorable, but like most children we put more emphasis on opening gifts than the meaning of Christmas.

Together we tore the wrapping paper from our new doll and admired it for a few moments. I thanked my parents and then asked, "Can I open the other present?"

"Since your sister is older, Huldah, let's allow her do it," Dad said.

My lips twisted with disgust as Beulah sat the box on her lap. But as soon as she began to delve inside, my eyes leaped to attention. After all, I reasoned, the gift itself is more important than the privilege of shedding the wrapping paper. Beulah lifted one roller skate from the container, and I confiscated the other. I surrendered the skate to my sister so she could fasten them onto the soles of her shoes. Then it was my turn. Mother could see I was perturbed that the skates were more suited to Beulah's feet than mine.

"Don't worry, Huldah. The skates can be made bigger or smaller with a key." I drooled with excitement at the thought of having my turn to use the skates. I had grown accustomed to being the younger daughter, exercising patience, and being the recipient of hand-me-downs. Beulah received many of her clothes from a girl in the church, and when she had outgrown them, naturally, they were passed on to me.

"Let's pray," Father said, disrupting my self-centered dreams. "Dear heavenly Father, thank You for giving our family shelter, food, and clothing. During these difficult times, we have never gone without. Thank You for giving the girls this pair of skates and doll. And God, we ask not for ourselves this Christmas but that in the coming days You would bless us with larger mission facilities and that our church would grow so we can help many more who do not know You. Amen."

Dad, a bold, boisterous man, always made sure that we understood the goodness of God. He also took a special interest in developing a strong relationship with my sister and me. Because of that, even though we were often left alone while our parents dealt with church-related business, we never felt neglected. We knew we were loved, and that's what mattered the most.

As a minister's wife, Mother sacrificed monetary gain and the tangible treasures other women had, but she was always faithful and content. I never heard her complain. She worked tirelessly at the church and in the community. Because of her many obligations, she was not always at home when we returned from school. We often found a list of chores and instructions for preparing dinner left on the table.

Dad and Mother tried to make up for their absence by taking us on special outings and picnics. As a family, we especially enjoyed the shopping trips to Bellingham, Washington. Between my bouts with car sickness, Beulah and I contemplated what we wanted to buy with our allowances.

Even the weekend allowances that our parents gave us occasionally were sacrificial gifts. Rather than receiving a salary, my parents lived on free-will church offerings, which were often barely adequate for us to rent an older house near my school.

During my first year of school, Beulah had to escort me to and from class. I was a mischievous, spirited child who wanted to talk to everyone and explore everything from neighborhood pets to precious flowers. Classrooms were too confining. On two occasions I liberated myself from what I deemed a penitentiary and fled home; Beulah had to be called from her class to locate me. In time, however, I learned to enjoy school and could be trusted to stay in my class and be well-behaved.

As I grew more responsible, I started spending my lunch periods off campus with my grandmother. Her house was directly across the street from the school I attended, and we both enjoyed this special time. Because of her stomach ailment, Grandma ate very little and could only attend church on Sunday mornings. My visits seemed to brighten her afternoon, especially since Uncle Lionel worked during the day for a real estate-insurance firm.

Every noon-hour, as I pranced through the screen door, she routinely asked, "Uldah, did you have a good morning at school?" Her gentle English accent always made me feel warm and secure.

"Yes, Grandma," I answered as I ran to her side.

Although Grandma always seemed to be at a loss for energy, somehow I thought her health problems were only temporary, a discomfort that would eventually disappear like the hovering clouds. Surely God doesn't need both my Grandpa and my Grandma, I thought.

# 4
# *Horseshoe Bay*

A family in our church owned a cottage on Horseshoe Bay, an ocean resort not far from Vancouver, Canada. They graciously permitted us to use the facility whenever we wanted, so at every opportunity Dad loaded us in the car for a getaway to this wonderland of sorts.

The cottage was three blocks from a wharf with curio shops, fishing boats, and fish and chip restaurants. I loved watching sea gulls glide through the salty air and fishermen carry their poles over their shoulders. Most of the time, children could be seen pulling their mother's arm, racing for the roped-off swimming area.

I had never been taught how to swim, but I was anxious to learn. One afternoon while Dad was at the other side of the wharf renting a fishing boat, I sauntered onto a dock without his supervision. As I stared into the rippling, blue water, the waves seemed to speak to me. "Come in and have some fun. There's no danger. Your father will never know."

Perspiration trickled down the channels of my palms as the sun's rays stung my bare arms. "Come in and have fun," the water sang again. Without further thought, I belly flopped into the ocean. As my hands broke the plane of the water, immediately regret flooded me. Thoughts of the biblical Jonah raced through my mind. The ocean swallowed my body, and I fell swiftly into the darkened depths of its stomach. Finally, my paddling legs shot me to the surface. That first gasp of air filled my burning lungs as I thrashed through the water.

Moments later, Dad and Beulah stood on the dock, watching me pull my dripping body up onto the shore. Beulah sternly scolded, "Huldah, you can't swim. You could have drowned."

I looked up, trying to construct the saddest, sorriest face imaginable.

Dad said nothing.

I hesitated for a few more seconds before pantomiming my excuse. "I couldn't help it. I wanted to swim."

Dad said, "Young lady, you could have drowned. Do you know that? Didn't I tell you to stay away from the water unless we were with you?"

Cleverly, I kept my eyes focused on the ground, away from my accuser.

"You know better than this. You don't know how to swim yet. Why did you disobey me?"

"I'm sorry," I fluted. "But how will I learn to swim if I don't try? I did it. You saw me dog paddle to shore."

Father handed me a lasting stare as if waiting for me to lift my head and meet his eyes before proceeding with his verbal lashing. Even though my pupils were about to burst, I managed to blink them upright then back to the ground, out of the reach of his scalding glare.

Shaking his head with disgust, Dad gently grabbed my wet hand and led me like an organ grinder's monkey back to the cottage.

After changing into some dry clothes, Dad took my sister and me fishing in a rented boat. He gave us emphatic orders to be quiet while his hook was in the water. And after what I had been through that morning, I was determined to obey.

The crescent moon hung low in the sky that evening when our boat came to shore. It was the bluest night sky I had ever seen. Except for the chattering crickets and glinting stars, one would have thought it was moments before daybreak.

Marching to the cottage—Beulah and me flanking Dad on each side—I finally garnered the courage I had sought all afternoon.

"I'm sorry for jumping in the water," I said.

Father shifted his rod to his other hand and patted me on the head. "I know you are. I love you and Beulah and just don't want you to get hurt. That's all."

That night, lying in bed, I thanked God for not letting me drown, for keeping me from getting a whipping, and for giving me the best father and mother in the whole world.

Having to leave Horseshoe Bay to return to our humble home always depressed me. We enjoyed our getaways at the cottage so much that sometimes I wished we could live there.

Following one holiday at the Bay, we discovered our house had been robbed while we were away. Mother opened the front door only to find drawers pulled out, closets in disarray, and many items missing.

Tears began to surface in Mother's eyes, but they quickly submerged. She always had such courage in the wake of disappointing circumstances. Dad called the police. Beulah and I ran to inspect our room and breathed a sigh of relief to find that, although clothes had been flung across the floor, nothing was taken.

Not long after the robbery Dad brought home a large black retriever named Don to guard our home and possessions against future intrusions. The dog was not very cordial and took great pleasure in scaring strangers. Dad warned us that the animal had a temper when provoked, but we soon discovered our new companion really loved to play with us. After Don came to live with us, we didn't mind staying alone as much.

At an early age I developed a love for my family and the security of home. I even missed my sister when we were separated. Some evenings when I intended to stay overnight at a friend's house, I had to call Dad to pick me up before bedtime. When homesickness suddenly overwhelmed me, nothing my hosts could say or do kept me from returning to my own bed.

Since Beulah was three years older, she had her own set of friends and her own agenda of activities. We sang together and shared a bed, but she was always a few steps ahead of me when it came to sophistication and maturity. She never appeared discombobulated or untidy. I viewed Beulah as a Cinderella with the IQ of a college professor. Most nights, as we slid under our covers, I launched questions into her ears. Even if she didn't have answers to my questions, she often formulated an explanation to repel my inquisitiveness and let her get to sleep.

During the summer, Beulah and I were separated when we took turns spending a week with Auntie Annie and her husband, Uncle Frank, and their two grown children, Wes and Irene. Uncle Frank helped run a family-owned furniture business in Vancouver, so they were affluent enough to treat us like princesses by taking us to ice cream shops and giving us gifts.

I didn't mind being away from my family when I was with the Hammonds; I always had so much fun. My only regret was that my parents made me take my violin along with instructions to practice one hour each day. At times I wanted to purposely misplace the instrument, but my parents had made too great a sacrifice to rent it for me.

My violin teacher, Mr. Greenaway, was scrupulous and demanding. He spent lesson after lesson trying to perfect fingering techniques that I considered trivial.

"Huldah," he admonished me each week, "if you don't practice, you will never be a fine violinist."

Some days when I lifted the wonderfully carved instrument to my chin, a grudging spirit would overcome me. I often fought the temptation to smash it into kindling. When I was at the Hammonds, I got away with playing the instrument in some of the strangest positions just to meet the practice time requirements: on my back in bed, on the floor with my legs folded, or just walking around the house.

My real musical love was singing. My voice teacher recognized my potential and invited me to tour Europe with a select choir made up of his students. But when the permission slip dropped from my father's hand into the waste paper basket, his answer was loud and clear . . . "No!"

"But Dad, why can't I go?" I pleaded, trying to revive my shrunken dreams. "I'm one of the lucky ones. Please let me go."

"My answer is no!"

I knew my father only too well. When he said "no" in that tone, he meant it. Incredulity grew in my face as my voice trailed off.

The voice teacher sent another letter home to my parents a few days later that further detailed his need for a high soprano voice like mine, but Dad staunchly held his ground and refused to change his mind.

Some time later, Mother clarified the motive behind Dad's climactic decision. She said he was afraid I might become an entertainer like he once was—a highlander dancer in Scotland—and would forget God and the ministry. Mother also relayed their hopes that I would be the one to carry on the family's tradition of ministers. Again I grit my teeth at the thought.

Dad didn't know it, but I disliked being the child of a preacher. I especially abhorred the high expectations and countless restrictions.

# 5
## *The Pastor's Daughter*

As the pastor's daughter, I wasn't permitted to get into trouble, especially at church. "She's such a darling girl. She's the apple of her father's eye." That's what the older women in our church said when I skipped to the front row, my sandy blond hair bouncing, my puffed-out dress swishing from side to side. Those same ladies would have sought my father's impeachment if they had known some of my fiendish activities: sticking gum under the pews and writing notes to friends during Dad's sermons.

When I was younger, several instances tarnished my crystal image. Dad, during church, had to cut short a sentence to correct my mischievous behavior. Breathing air through his teeth, he pointed his bayonet-sized finger at me and warned, "Huldah, you are disrupting this service. I want you to come over here immediately and sit on the front seat—and don't say another word."

Then when we arrived home from church, I heard an encore performance of the same speech. Only, in private, he used a leather belt to emphasize his point. I used to hide his belts, but I soon learned my schemes were lessons in futility. He had a vast supply.

Being a preacher's daughter was like being a princess in a swarm of newspaper reporters. My every phrase and every gesture were scrutinized. Along with the red-carpet limelight came ridiculing critics—church members who relished the chance to dislodge the tiara from my head. Members of the church expected me to be the epitome of the perfect child: sinless, obedient, and mannerly.

Attendance at the evangelistic center began to flourish as I entered my teens. This occurred largely because of my parents' sacrifice and hard work and their willingness to evangelize the community. Their evangelism activities were, in actuality, an embarrassment to me. I agonized over having to participate in their outdoor street meetings near Woodward's department store where Mother played the hand organ and Dad preached. I, meanwhile, did my best to hide behind anything that could shield me from public view. The thought of being teased by my classmates if they spotted me was too much for me to bear.

My appreciation for Dad's occupation wavered, at times feeling proud, other times resentful. Since the church was in a portion of town relegated to the poor and destitute, I was ashamed to tell my friends at school where my father pastored. The sidewalks were dirty, and many of the buildings had broken windows and crumbling interiors.

My pride also despised having to wear hand-me-downs—a stigma of being a preacher's daughter—when other children came to church and school modeling new outfits. I truly admired my parents' unfailing dedication to the church, and I appreciated their willingness to go without so we could have something new on occasion; nevertheless, at an early age I vowed never to enter the ministry because I was unwilling to pay so great a price.

The church people were generous to Beulah and me, especially at Christmas when they normally lavished us with presents and homemade treats. I think they felt sorry for us, as if we were destitute orphans at the mercy of their pocketbooks. Early in Dad's ministry there were times when we needed financial help. But I disliked having to depend on others, and the older I became the more I sought to be independently secure.

Two elderly women in the church were especially fond of my sister and me. Quite often Mrs. Dawson and Mrs. Taylor brushed by us in the sanctuary after the service and stuck a coin or two into our palms to express their affection. One year Beulah and I made a pact to save whatever money they gave us and combine it with some of our lunch money so we could buy our parents a nice gift for Christmas. I'll never forget the shock in Mother's and Dad's eyes when we presented them with a complete dinner set of bone china. I can't remember ever seeing them so dumbfounded, wondering how we had paid for such an expensive gift.

When the congregation started to exceed the building's capacity, Father began praying in earnest for new facilities. Fortunately, as far as I was concerned, God chose to give us a newer home in a nicer neighborhood before He gave us a new church. A layman helped my parents with the down payment so they could purchase the house.

Walking into the two-bedroom house on 18th Avenue West for the first time did wonders for my self-esteem. I could now invite friends to our house without embarrassment. I felt like God was finally giving us "something" for my parents' labors. In spite of the new home, however, I didn't change my mind about avoiding the ministry.

On a pleasant Saturday evening, Mother and I were relaxing in the kitchen. She was studying her Sunday School lesson, and I was sitting at the table wishing tomorrow wasn't Sunday. We had services all day, and Dad allowed us to read only the Bible or Sunday school literature on the Sabbath. We weren't even permitted to play outside or buy an ice cream cone.

This particular Saturday night, Mother, Beulah, and I were still exhausted from having spent most of the day peeling and canning pears. Suddenly, a tremendous crash reverberated from the cellar. It sounded like our house had caved in completely.

"What was that?" I asked gravely, wanting to disbelieve that our day's work had just fallen from the shelves.

Mother's eyes returned to her Sunday school lesson. "I don't know," she said matter-of-factly, as though she knew but wasn't overly concerned.

I could just visualize a heap of glass and fruit below, so I asked, "Don't you want me to go down and see what happened?"

Mother paused for a few breaths before she said, "Huldah, tomorrow's Sunday, the Lord's day; whatever it is can wait until Monday."

I couldn't believe what I had just heard.

She stood, bolted the door to the cellar, and said, "We'll worry about it later. No use ruining the Lord's day."

I asked rhetorically, "After all of our hard work, why did this have to happen?"

Mother opened her Bible and read me a verse. ". . . [take] joyfully the spoiling of your goods" (Hebrews 10:34, KJV).

Naturally I had to ponder that phrase a few minutes, trying to determine what good could come from this disaster and why I had to be joyful about it.

At that moment I realized just how religious and righteous my parents were. Despite my occasional disagreements with Dad, I respected him as the devout, honest constable of our home. Mother warranted equal regard, even though she was soft spoken and had a more gentle walk with God.

As I watched her gleaning from the Bible that evening, it occurred to me that I would never be as "spiritual" as my parents. I would never reach their level of "holiness" or discipline. I feared I would always fall short of their expectations.

Dad and Mother thrived on being in church services all the time. On the other hand, I had trouble accepting the value of spending almost every spare moment in church. I knew it was important, but I had to discover the value of church for myself. Some Sundays, notwithstanding the frequent midweek services, I felt like I had a ball and chain fastened to my ankle as I entered the "religious" stockade. Our "day of rest" was anything but relaxing; it consisted of an early morning prayer meeting, a morning worship service, a short lunch break at the church, a Sunday school hour, an afternoon service, and an evening rally.

Beulah and I often sang duets and performed in the orchestra, so our attendance was mandatory. I played my violin, and Beulah played the saxophone. Her childhood friend and eventual husband, Bob Dobson, played the trombone. On Sunday evenings when the service extended into the late hours, Uncle Lionel dropped my sister and me off at our home so we could get to sleep at a decent hour.

On Wednesdays we seldom spoke with Mother. That was her day of prayer and fasting at the mission. Although I often wished she was at home, I marveled at her stamina and devotion.

Our Saturday evenings were spent at CKMO, the local radio station, where Dad broadcasted his weekly program "The Vesper Hour." The broadcast opened with a selection of "He Careth for You" from the thirty voice "Vesper Choir." Then Dad, in his rich voice, announced to the listeners, "Now 'Little Huldah' will come and sing for us." Uncle Lionel played the accompaniment on the piano.

The program reached into Washington and stretched eastward through Canada. We received many requests for hymns from listeners, so frequently both Beulah and I had to learn new songs. With each passing year, I renewed my vow to dodge a life of full-time ministry. Huldah Munroe would never marry a preacher, but I didn't have the heart to tell my parents.

# 6
# *A Bright Future*

If there was one thing I disliked about school, it was report cards. Beulah was always so eager to showcase her outstanding grades. I, on the other hand, did all I could to conceal my marks. When I had delayed the inevitable and had exhausted every plausible excuse for its absence, I would be forced to surrender the card for my parents' inspection. I usually left the room while they surveyed the edict of doom, knowing full well my name would soon be reverberating from Dad's lips.

"Huldah, come here. Huldah!"

At that moment I could have crawled down to the cellar and lived happily with the spiders for a week.

"Huldah, what have you been doing to get grades like this?" He waved the report card in front of my face like a paper fan.

"I'm trying my best."

"You're too smart to get grades like this. You're not trying. Otherwise, your grades would be as good as your sister's."

I didn't respond.

"What are we going to do about this? I don't want to see grades like these again. Do you understand me?"

"Yes. But I'm still above a C-average, and I'm doing well in physical education and music."

"Look at your math grade. You can do better than that."

"Mr. Smith is mean to me. I'm afraid of him. He slaps my wrist with a ruler if I make a mistake."

"It looks like I'm going to have to do more than slap your wrist if you don't improve. It's obvious you're not doing your best. I know you can do better."

"I'll try harder," I said in the form of a confession.

"Good," he said, his stern expression transforming into a smile. "I just want you to understand the importance of school. You should be playing less sports so you can study and get straight A's like Beulah and have a bright future."

I loved to participate in grass hockey, baseball, swimming, ice and roller skating, and many other sports. Whenever Dad mentioned "sports" and "future" in the same sentence, I braced myself for another lecture about the ministry God had for me and the dangers of becoming preoccupied with athletics.

Mediocre report cards had a way of inciting Dad's wrath, which often manifested itself in the form of a stinging lecture. I listened intently, even though I could nearly predict his speeches word for word. Mother seldom became involved in disciplining my sister and me; she left that to my father. His anger, however, was always short-lived. Two hours after getting spanked for my misdeeds, I could be seen fishing with my father.

My parents, to their credit, balanced their admonishments by applauding our accomplishments. When I was in seventh grade, I won an oratorical contest in which three thousand students from grades seven to twelve competed. I was awarded the first place medal for my speech, "Life in Japan." After he read about it in the newspaper, Father didn't try to hide his pride. He kept that clipping in his desk for many years and was never bashful about showing it to guests. Somehow, that seemed to make up for my less than outstanding academic marks.

Entering Fairview High from Kitsilano Junior High School was a major leap toward womanhood. Before I set one foot on the grounds as a student, Dad repeated his rules against becoming too friendly with non-Christian boys. He said, "If you date them once, you may end up marrying them. So don't put yourself in that predicament by disobeying your parents and God."

One day Dad spotted me walking home from school with a boy named Gerry. Dad pulled his car to the side of the road and gave me one stiff glare as if to say, "Disobedient child, get in this car right now!" I was surprised when he didn't utter a word of rebuke the entire drive home. I guess he knew I had understood his message "loud and clear."

Gerry, one of the most popular kids in school, was fun to be with and a fine athlete. He had light brown hair and a tan that looked like he had been raised on the beaches of Waikiki. We served on the youth council together, and I often watched him play soccer before school. He invited me to various school functions, but out of loyalty to my Dad's rules I declined—most of the time.

Ice skating was becoming a popular sport in Vancouver, and all the students frequented the local rink. Since the loudspeakers played waltz music, however, Dad felt skating was too much like dancing. Therefore, he said, the rink was not a proper environment for Christians. Dad forbid us to go because his daughters needed to set an example for the other young people in the church.

One afternoon I joined a few teenagers from the church and sneaked off to the rink. Dad never would have discovered my disobedience if I hadn't been so lucky and won a free book of tickets at the rink. Somehow they found their way into Dad's hands.

"Where did these come from?" he asked, waving the tickets in my face—a face that quickly lost all color.

At a loss for words, I stood there feeling foolish.

"Huldah, I asked you a question."

The temptation to lie ran through my mind, but I knew Dad was too smart to be fooled. I cleared my throat, thinking quickly.

Dad's patience waned during the oozing lull of silence. "Why did you go? Some people in the church told me you were there. Why did you disobey me?"

I was suddenly grateful I hadn't lied.

"I went because I like to skate. I went with friends from the church."

Confession *is* good for the soul, yet I wasn't about to tell him about Gerry being there, too.

"Didn't I tell you not to go there?"

"Yes, but all my friends go."

"That doesn't mean you can. They look up to you, so if you go they think it's all right, too. And I've told you," he paused, "it's no place for a Christian to spend her time."

"But there's nothing wrong with it. It doesn't hurt me."

With displeasure nearly drained from his voice, he said, "You heard me."

Not being able to understand the evil he found in skating rinks, I went to my room. With a pillow wrapped around my head, I said, "Why did I have to be a preacher's daughter? We never get to do anything! Everyone else can have fun, but we have to spend most of our time at church."

I stayed in my room for a long while feeling sorry for myself, thinking about everything I had to sacrifice because of my parents' convictions. I thought about my second-hand clothing and Mother's strict sentiments against makeup. I was at least grateful they allowed us to keep in step with the fashions of the day.

"I can't wait until I can buy my own things," I said into my pillow.

When Beulah left for school or work, I used to rummage through her closet for clothing that fit me. One day I wore the prized brown blazer Dad had bought for her. At school, I was enjoying the compliments of my friends until I leaned too far over the paper-cutter and sliced through one of the blazer's lapels. When I came home, I was too scared to make a confession. I hung the blazer where I had found it and braced myself each morning for Beulah's inevitable reaction. It took me quite a while to save enough money to buy her a new one.

A lady in our church orchestra who played the violin next to me was the object of my envy. I always admired and observed her fashions, unknowingly becoming paranoid about my own clothing and lack thereof. I so wanted to have a pair of open toed, slingback shoes like she had, but I couldn't gather the courage to ask Dad.

"He'll object anyway, so what's the use?" I told myself. But Dad surprised me when he agreed to give me the money to purchase the shoes of my choice.

My first encounter with makeup wasn't as favorable. My girlfriends and I had put on makeup and lipstick at school and went to the Aristocrat—a hamburger and ice cream hangout near our high school. The juke box was raging when we crawled into our booth and placed our orders. An evangelist, who was in town speaking for my father, just happened to walk in with his wife. He took one look at me, smiled, and sat down in a booth nearby. I wished I could have hid my blushing face behind a menu. Even the makeup could not camouflage my embarrassment. My lips must have resembled a bleeding tomato.

I had envisioned him going directly to my parents to testify against me, but my fears were never realized. Later that night, as I sat in the choir behind the evangelist, my saintly face beamed with its natural color. My heart was both relieved and grateful that he had not divulged what he had witnessed.

My first job was at Woodward's department store during their "99 Cent Days." Once a month, during the sale, all the merchandise sold for 99 cents. Because of the flood of customers the sale attracted, I was hired for $1.70 a day to work in the wool department. My wages weren't high, but I wasn't complaining. Once I started working, I developed a deeper appreciation for money and how it could benefit one's appearance. I began saving whatever I could just to elevate my wardrobe.

During this period of high unemployment, I considered myself fortunate just to have a job, albeit marginal employment at best. During my Christmas vacation, I worked part-time in Woodward's men's furnishings department. Beulah had been working there for some time and had already begun climbing the ladder of success. Eventually she became private assistant to the general manager of the entire store.

I began studying stenography and bookkeeping in school and later landed a summer secretarial job with the University of British Columbia in the School of Forestry. My most auspicious opportunity, however, came during my senior year of high school when Uncle Lionel helped me get a job as secretary in the Land Registry Department at the provincial court house.

Once Beulah and I worked regularly, Dad required us to pay room and board, all in the name of teaching us an appreciation for money and budgeting. I must admit, at first I was skeptical of his explanation, perceiving it as an excuse. But his honest intentions soon came into view; he gave us far more than what we paid him each month. The older we grew, the more financially secure my parents were, and they were able to buy us gifts unlike anything we received as children.

When Dad finally purchased a cottage at Deep Cove, a suburb of Vancouver, it was God's way of rewarding his years of sacrifice and effort. Never had I seen my father so proud as the day he announced, "It's all ours."

Don, our dog, liked Deep Cove because it gave him room to roam. I remember his ears flapping and his tongue wagging as he darted across a field like an African leopard. Beulah and I liked playing badminton there and torpedoing across the water in the motor boat Dad bought after we had owned the property for a while.

Nothing was as satisfying and relaxing to Dad as going fishing. He always wanted me to go with him because, I guess, he considered me the boy of the family. I didn't exactly enjoy fishing, however, primarily because I had to keep my lips sealed. Dad said any talking would scare the fish away. I didn't mind reeling in fish; but it was difficult to keep my mouth shut between "bites." I also didn't relish having to endure Dad's sermonettes about my future and the value of entering the ministry as we traveled to and from the lake.

My father's propaganda concerning the rewards of "full-time service" never infiltrated my wall of fears, though. My aspirations held no room for poverty and sacrifice like my parents had suffered through.

Even though I was on the student council, president of the senior class, president of the Bible club, and a member of the baseball, hockey, and swimming teams, Dad still restricted me from attending any of the school functions where dancing was permitted.

Once I reached the edge of womanhood, Dad became less strict about some things. My Sunday schedule wasn't as monopolized, and I began to date. Dad still enforced a 10:00 p.m. curfew, however. On Saturday nights, the radio program concluded at nine so I still had an official hour of freedom left. Since that didn't give me much time, I was often an hour or two late. The way I figured it, a reprimand was a small price to pay if it meant spending more time with a new boyfriend.

# 7
# *Marry a Preacher? Not Me!*

Several boys had expressed the depth of their affection for me, but, awkwardly, I couldn't bring myself to tell them I loved them, too. That was a phrase I had reserved for my husband-to-be, and I wasn't ready to make that commitment to anyone.

There were nights I laid in bed and repeated to myself, "Huldah Smith, Huldah Jones, Huldah Nelson, Huldah Peters." The mere thought of marriage prompted nervous giggles to erupt from my throat. But, invariably, I fell asleep wondering who I would marry and questioning God's will for my life.

I often said to myself, Marry a preacher? Never in a million years! I had seen the wives of too many struggling evangelists and ministers to consider putting myself through that type of torture. In particular, the memory of Miss Gail, a missionary to Japan, was enough to forever dissuade me from the ministry. Her clothes were tattered, she was very thin, and she told ghastly stories depicting the "abnormal" conditions in which she lived. I still remembered waving goodby as her ship set sail for Japan, and thinking, "I could never bring myself to live that way."

I didn't want to disappoint my parents; nor did I want to suffer. I just wanted a "normal" life.

Since Beulah was already engaged to Bob, Dad issued a sales pitch about his youngest daughter to every unmarried evangelist or minister who held services at our church. I tolerated his meddling but became deeply agitated when I had to relinquish my room to these preachers who roamed the countryside like gypsies. Occasionally, I hid a brush or another pointed object in my bed to show my displeasure. Since I was paying room and board, I figured I deserved to sleep on something more comfortable than a lumpy couch.

Long before evangelist Mark Buntain came to our church, Father had built him up as a chivalrous prince. But, then again, Dad had issued similar advertisements for other young preachers who held a Bible and could quote volumes of verses. So I paid no attention to Dad's description of this visitor coming to hijack my bed.

The young evangelist's father, the Reverend Dan Buntain, was the General Superintendent of the Assemblies of God of Canada. The tall distinguished man occasionally hired me to do his typing when he was passing through our area. Pastor Buntain had written my father about scheduling services for his son Mark who was leaving his pastorate in Moose Jaw and embarking on the evangelistic field. Having heard about the son's preaching ability, Dad scheduled two weeks of meetings—although the revival was later extended to four weeks.

After much persuasion, I convinced Dad to let the young evangelist stay with another family in the church. That way I wouldn't have to move out of my bedroom. We did have him over for dinner, however, and Dad, in his usual fashion, brought out the family album to highlight pictures of me and my accomplishments. This was accompanied by subtle suggestions of my credentials to be a minister's wife.

The twenty-one-year-old evangelist was thoughtful and courteous, but there certainly weren't any romantic sparks shooting across the table between the two of us that evening. Besides, I had just ended a serious relationship with another young man.

Having grown up in church, I considered myself a critic of preaching styles and deliveries. Mark Buntain's preaching was on the unusual side, but no one could doubt his intensity and effectiveness. Rarely had I heard ministers who possessed his fervency and conviction. Hand wavers, finger pointers, and foot stampers were common, but this young man stirred our congregation more with his words than any of his physical gestures.

That night, his message, "The Choice for Your Life," touched my heart and melted away all my self-conscious concerns about what people in the congregation would think. Unhesitatingly, I followed others to the altar and began to sob. For years I had been dictating to God what I wanted for my life. As I knelt, it became apparent that God had a different course for my future than the direction I had plotted. Stubbornly, I argued with God at the altar, bargaining for a better lot in life. The more I prayed, the more I wept.

I'm sure my parents and other parishioners wondered what had prompted such an emotional outburst. At that moment, what they thought didn't matter. I was negotiating with God, hoping He would retract His calling on my life to the ministry.

"God," I prayed silently, "I have lived most of my life sacrificially. I like nice things. Please don't ask me to be a preacher's wife. I'll do anything You ask, but please, God, not the ministry."

The longer I dwelt on the issue, the more I knew it was my Creator's compelling voice speaking. I couldn't doubt He had placed a special calling on my life.

# 8
# *Chocolates and Perfume*

As I stepped out into the warm summer sun, the red roses surrounding the court house beamed in contrast to the gray walls around my desk at the Land Registry office. As I descended the cobblestone steps, I was surprised to see Dad waiting for me. He was smiling as if greeting visitors on a Sunday morning at the back door of the church.

Since I had broken off a serious relationship with my boyfriend days earlier, my relationship with my parents had never been better. They had done their share of worrying about my future and were grateful for my decision. My parents seemed to have a new respect for me and no longer treated me like a school girl who had difficulty making up her mind.

"Hi," I said, "what brings you here?"

Dad flung his arm around my shoulder and said, "Mark is going to stay for another week, so I thought you might like to join us for lunch."

I accepted the invitation and sat through a multitude of stories about Mark's travels and meetings. The conversation wasn't that stimulating, but I had to confess I was intrigued by his dedication.

After the service that evening, Mark approached me in the back of the church.

"I enjoyed your message," I said before he could greet me.

"Thank you. Listen, would you like to go out for some Chinese food?"

I turned my head with woeful deliberation. I could sense my smile slowly changing into a flustered stare. My cheeks and forehead felt like they were dripping with sweat. I was afraid to go because then surely people in the church would think I had broken up with my boyfriend for Mark.

Although knowing their answer, I said, "I'll have to ask my parents."

"Your father has already agreed to loan me his car, so there'll be no problem."

I hesitated, searching for another excuse. With my forefinger cupping my chin, appearing again to be deep in meditation, I agreed to his proposition.

I felt like a teenager on her first date, unusually quiet and fidgety. Still, there was something romantic about the tranquil drive to the restaurant. Surprisingly, the silence was not threatening.

As soon as we walked into the Chinatown restaurant, Mark began speaking Chinese. He even ordered our meal in the waiter's native language. When Mark pastored in Moose Jaw, Saskatchewan, he had frequented a Chinese restaurant where the owner's son had taught him how to pronounce various Chinese words.

That night I learned he had been a radio broadcaster with his own program out of Chatham, Ontario. He had also joined the Royal Canadian Mounted Police but was discharged when God called him to pastor a small church on the Canadian prairies. While pastoring he had become friendly with a nurse. He confided, however, that his parents were against the relationship because they did not feel she would enhance Mark's ministry.

I asked, "Do you want to travel as an evangelist the rest of your life?"

"Actually, I don't know what God has for me. Sometimes I think I'd like to serve as a missionary, maybe in China so I can put what I've learned to work."

"Well, one thing's for sure, you wouldn't have any trouble ordering your food," I quipped, though sensing his deep love for the Chinese people.

When I rolled onto my pillow that evening, I realized the mythical veil between myself and the ministry was rending, almost as if God had sent Mark Buntain to disarm me of my fears of being a minister's wife.

The last night of Mark's revival, he had once again invited me to join him for a snack afterwards. Waiting for the lengthy message to end that blustery evening was like crossing a barren desert. Throughout his sermon, I felt my eyes drawn to the pulpit like never before as I studied his shoes, pants, shiny tie, ironed shirt, and the strands of hair that occasionally fell onto his forehead.

He seemed to pray for everyone at the altar twice before we finally departed for the drive-in restaurant. I waited with remarkable patience. I realized then that I had a growing admiration for Mark, but to get too friendly with such a zealous preacher was another question altogether.

At the restaurant, Mark's personality revealed itself like a beautiful statue being carved right before my eyes. This serious, mature preacher exhibited a delightful boyish charm that previously had been shielded from my view. Mark Buntain was captivating. His humorous stories and wit were beginning to win my affection.

Then, just as my heart was melting, I spilled a soft drink into his lap. Embarrassment breezed across my face. Rather than reach for a napkin, he began soaking up the excess with his handkerchief.

"I'm so sorry. Please don't ruin your hanky," I said.

"You're worth it," he said with a grin.

Instantly, I deduced he had an interest in me, too. But just as my hopes began to soar, they came crashing down like those of a rejected waif. I realized we would be separated for months without an opportunity to become better acquainted. His meetings would take him across Canada and the United States into churches with many attractive, eligible girls. I would quickly fade from his mind.

A few days following his departure, Mark phoned after hearing me sing on Dad's radio program. I then knew he hadn't forgotten me and he, too, sensed something special about our budding friendship.

Whatever questions I had about his feelings were answered when a box arrived from Mark. My heart flip-flopped as I read his name on the package. Inside were a box of name brand chocolates and a bottle of expensive perfume.

That night I went to bed saying to myself, "Huldah Buntain, Huldah Buntain, Huldah Buntain." And, somehow, this time I knew it was for real.

# 9
# *Falling in Love*

Mark's Saturday evening phone calls became the pinnacle of my week. He shared about his services and traveling experiences and issued romantic reminders of his fond feelings. His life seemed more exciting, yet traveling from church to church and sleeping in pastor's homes and church apartments still wasn't appealing to me.

I yearned to be with him, but surrendering the security of my job and home held me back. I knew I was falling in love, but I wasn't certain it was worth the discomfort of traveling constantly, which I knew would be my lot if I got serious with Mark Buntain.

Maybe he won't ask me to marry him, I thought to myself. Maybe my feelings are deeper than his.

But my parents were bent on seeing this courtship sprout into marriage. "He's the one," they often remarked. And when the phone rang on Saturdays after Dad's radio program, Mother would declare, "There's my future son-in-law."

Whenever Mark's meetings brought him close to Vancouver, he would visit briefly. But when he traveled four days by train just to be with us for Christmas and to attend Beulah and Bob's wedding, I knew he really cared for me.

"Huldah, do you love me?" Mark asked as the two of us sat on the couch in our living room one night.

"Yes," I answered.

"Even though I'm going to be an evangelist? I don't feel called to be a pastor, you know."

At that moment nothing mattered but being with him, and I told him so.

We kissed and embraced, and, unregrettably, I committed myself to him and the evangelistic field even though we weren't as yet engaged.

Dominion Day, July 1, Mark met me in Vancouver for our church's annual picnic. We took a boat to a park where we spent the day playing softball and participating in races. When we returned that evening, with our faces sun-burned and our hair stringing out wildly, we discovered that Mark's mother, sister, and brother-in-law were in town hoping to meet the girl who had captured his affections.

Mark and I tried to make ourselves presentable by caking burn cream on our faces and running a brush through our hair before driving over to their motel. We still resembled a pair of backpackers who had just returned from a week-long camping trip.

Ed, Mark's brother-in-law, opened the door and broke the ice. "So this must be the marvelous Huldah we've heard so much about." Ed's smile was one of the widest and most genuine I had ever seen.

Then Mark's sister, Alice, a pretty girl with an olive complexion, put her arms around me as if to welcome me to the family. "Mark tells us you're the most wonderful girl he's ever met," she said.

Mark and I blushed simultaneously, although our faces were already bright red.

Mrs. Buntain stepped in front of me and her eyes scanned me from top to bottom as if she were standing in front of a full-length mirror.

Kindly she said, "Mark has told me all about you. You come from a lovely family."

"Thank you," I said. "It's nice to meet all of you."

Mrs. Buntain was an intense, intelligent woman who had taught school for many years. Groomed to perfection, her every hair fell into place. She had a reputation for being exceedingly generous but very opinionated. I studied her like a pupil learning from a mentor. She carried herself with such dignity. Mark gave her a firm hug, then stepped back to admire her.

I didn't get well acquainted with Mrs. Buntain until I stayed with her at Langly Prairie, where Mark was invited to speak at a youth camp meeting. Mrs. Buntain, Alice, and Ed had gone to the camp to spend the week with Mark, and I joined them for the weekend.

We had plenty of opportunities during that time to share, and I was confident I was winning Mrs. Buntain's trust. Then, during the second night that I was with her, she grabbed her lower abdomen in pain. I wasn't sure what was happening. I scurried from one cabin to the other trying to find Ed, Alice, or Mark, calling their names into windows and throughout the wooded surroundings. Finally Ed and Alice answered and raced Mrs. Buntain to the hospital, where her ailment was diagnosed as a gall bladder attack.

Summer, fall, and winter linked together like one unpredictable season. Ed and Alice were traveling with Mark on the evangelistic field, so it was consoling to know Alice was caring for her brother. I dreamed of the day *I* would join the team. Somehow my concerns about poverty and living in church apartments weren't as important now. All I knew was I wanted to be Mrs. Buntain, regardless of any undesirable demands accompanying the title.

Although I didn't know it, Mark had already purchased a ring. While my father had given Mark his blessing, he had one requirement—that we wait until I turned twenty. Dad knew Mark was lonely on the road and, therefore, let me marry sooner than he would have permitted otherwise.

We were sitting on the couch in our living room when Mark proposed. He said, "This has been the most wonderful year of my life. I love you; will you marry me?"

Before I had even uttered a word, Mark presumptuously lifted the ring box from his pocket. He slipped a diamond that was far beyond his means onto my finger. I must have studied that beautiful stone from every angle over the next few minutes.

Mark's father had tested his son's devotion to me by telling him he could buy a second hand ring at a fraction of the price. Mark opposed the idea, but Pastor Buntain took him to a pawn shop anyway. Mark was unaware that I had done work for his father and knew him well, so he took his father's teasing seriously, insisting he was in love with me and that he wanted the best ring he could buy—certainly not a second hand one.

Eventually his father took him to an exclusive jewelry store in Edmonton. "Miss," Mark's father said to the salesgirl, "show my son the best diamond ring you have because he wants to give it to a wonderful girl."

Pastor Buntain changed his travel schedule to be in Vancouver the night Mark gave me the ring. I realized this great man of God, whom I had admired through the years as a folk hero, would soon be my father-in-law. But I knew there would be plenty of time to get used to my new family and wearing a ring from a man I loved.

Throughout the night I must have lifted the ring to my eyes twenty times. I could hardly sleep as thoughts of the day and the future raced through my mind.

The next thirteen months were agonizing, wanting to be with Mark, yet regretting the notion of leaving home. As the November wedding date approached, Mother had mixed emotions as well. She loved Mark; so did my father, but they knew how terribly they would miss me.

One weekend before we were married I went to Linden, Washington to hear Mark preach. I was bursting with pride when Mark introduced me from the pulpit as the "soon-to-be Mrs. Buntain." That night I suddenly realized I was destined to become just what my mother had been all these years—a faithful, supportive minister's wife. The more I thought about it, the more I felt as though I might drown in responsibility.

# 10
## *Paradise*

Wednesday, November 22, 1944. I had never seen so many friends in one place. Thankfully, the stormy weather had not dissuaded them from coming to our wedding. Mother feared our church would not have adequate seating capacity, so the ceremony was held at Mt. Pleasant Baptist Church.

As I peeked at the audience minutes before the start of the music that night, my stomach was tumbling slowly but under control. In the dressing room, the flower girl was jumping around nervously, and the attendants were trying to sponge mud spots out of their dresses just before we walked the aisle—mud collected while coming from home to the church.

Since Dad was officiating the wedding, Uncle Lionel escorted me down the aisle. When I entered the sanctuary, my hand was clasping Uncle Lionel's bent elbow tightly. Every eye was fixed on the center aisle as I made my gliding approach through the parting of the pews. Eyes, seemingly a million eyes, scanned my satin wedding gown. I was oblivious to the array of floral displays and organ music in the background. Suddenly, nestled between a group of navy blue suits, Mark's smile awakened me from my daze.

Our wedding was a resplendent ceremony fit for the climax of a best-selling novel. Alice sang beautifully, and Dad's segment was a masterpiece. Nothing pleased me more than the words "I now pronounce you man and wife." When Mark lifted the veil, what few swirling butterflies I felt were released. I walked down the aisle relieved and relaxed, with an aura that said I was proud to be Mrs. Mark Buntain.

After a beautiful reception, the wedding party formed a motorcade behind our chauffeured vehicle. The procession continued through town and to the docks where we boarded the Princess ship destined for Victoria. As we departed, family and friends showered us with confetti.

Mark had rented the honeymoon suite, where we would stay until the ship landed in Victoria early the next morning. Once we landed we would stay at the Empress Hotel. I would have been content staying aboard ship for the entire three days. The state room was beautifully designed with multi-pleated silken curtains—strictly for decoration—that swung across one complete wall. The Colonial bed was adorned with flawless linens and a heavily padded bedspread.

To my delight, the Old English hotel in Victoria was just as magnificent. Majestic ferns in brass pots lined the hallways and lobby. The crystal chandeliers were breathtaking. From our room on the fifth floor, we could look out over the city through the large arch windows like two pigeons desperately in love.

I was in paradise, but I knew a terrifying reality was only one day away. Tomorrow we would leave for Seattle, then on to our first revival meeting as husband and wife.

# 11
## Saint Mark

Mark had promised the Northwest District of the Assemblies of God that we would hold meetings in every church that opened its doors to us. But before our very first meeting in Auburn, Washington, I was already in tears. Just like when I was a child, homesickness crept in and blanketed me. I questioned whether I could live the life of a vagabond. Doubts and despair threatened to steal whatever composure I possessed.

Mark wrapped me in his arms and said, "It's okay, you'll get over it in time."

I wasn't so sure.

Then, like a panacea from heaven, Mark promised we could go back to Vancouver to visit my family for Christmas. My tears slowly subsided. I felt like a bawling child who had just gotten her wish.

Since we didn't have a car, the pastor of the church in Auburn had met us in Seattle and driven back to his church where we would be staying in their evangelist's apartment. It was a far cry from the Empress Hotel. The cubicle was upstairs at the front of the church. It contained a few pieces of furniture and a couch that converted into a bed.

The walls of the apartment were covered with Sunday school paraphernalia. On Sunday morning, we had to put our things away so the room could be used as a classroom. To use the bathroom, we had to travel down the stairs to the church foyer. And to bathe we had to jaunt down the block to the pastor's house.

To myself, I wondered if this was typical of the living quarters on the evangelistic field. The church was clean and well-kept, and the people were warm and friendly; this just wasn't the grandiose Empress Hotel, nor the Munroe home in Vancouver. Everything was so foreign. Uncomfortable. Certainly, I thought, this was much finer than some of the churches I had seen that resembled abandoned, decrepit barns found collapsing in the countryside.

In Auburn, though, we met the Stewart families—two brothers who married two sisters. They owned a farm, so during the revival they brought us meat, milk, and vegetables. They were so generous and understanding, commissioned by God to comfort a young girl coping with the prospects of a lonely, nomadic future.

Little did we know that Auburn would one day be our "home."

Mark had told me about Ed's propensity for practical jokes, so I watched him with cautious eyes when he and Alice joined us for a series of meetings in Burlington and Sedro Woolley, Washington.

One time when Ed, Alice, and Mark were traveling together, Ed phoned and told Mark he had been arrested for speeding. Naturally, Mark and Alice, who were cleaning the evangelist's apartment at the time, were startled by Ed's news. Within seconds Mark had hurled himself out the door and was barreling down the street to rescue his wayward brother-in-law.

To Mark's surprise, he found Ed standing outside a phone booth near a gas station. Instead of being arrested, Ed was having his car serviced and waiting for his preacher-chauffeur to arrive. Once again Mark had fallen for one of Ed's gimmicks.

Alice befriended me as a sister. We laundered clothes and talked by the hour while the men drove throughout the city announcing the nightly revival services on a portable loud-speaker system attached to Ed's car. The two of us talked about everything from having children to establishing a home. Even though the future was somewhat intimidating, being able to expose my fears to a woman who had similar concerns and aspirations was therapeutic.

Ed himself brought much needed comic relief. His tricks included waking Mark up by throwing spit-wads in his face and stuffing wet toilet paper down the back of his shirt. He even filled Mark's shoes with shaving cream. I didn't escape his innocent jabs either. "Hoodah," he announced, "I've been adding up all the weight you say you've lost, and I've come to the conclusion that you've disappeared."

Mark, meanwhile, was determined to even the score for all of us. Prior to an evening service, he put Limburger cheese in Ed's shoes. Throughout the meeting, children were hold-ing their noses, and wives were complaining to their hus-bands about the gagging, floating fragrance. When Ed slipped off his shoes later that night and took a whiff of his insoles, he nearly fell unconscious.

Alice and I roared with laughter, for this was so unlike Mark and so uncommon for someone to successfully play a trick on Ed.

Perhaps the most humorous event of our travels together took place when the four of us attempted to sing as a quar-tet. Alice possessed exceptional musical abilities, having studied voice and piano at a conservatory for seven years. Ed also sang quite well. Mark, on the other hand, we soon learned, had difficulty holding pitch. So, from then on we were a trio, and Mark was encouraged to concentrate on his preaching.

I hated to say farewell to Alice and Ed. In the short time we had been together, I had grown dependent on Alice for understanding and encouragement and on Ed for laughter. In the coming months, my husband and I would have only each other. The thought of both the unknown and the known responsibilities were disquieting to me.

Months later, we received a call from the pastor in Auburn, informing us of his intentions to take another pastorate and inviting Mark to come as his replacement. It sounded appealing to me—to cast an anchor from the trunk of our car and spend a year or two in one location—but Mark wasn't interested.

"It's not my calling," he said with finality.

With Mark's recommendation, however, Ed and Alice were offered the position.

Mark had no intentions of settling down. The evangelistic field was his frontier, and nothing would ever change that, I thought.

Making new friends at churches and having to leave them behind every two weeks quickly took its toll on me. I dreaded Saturdays, having to pull into a new town and get situated and wondering if the church would respond to our ministry. Evangelistic work was like enduring a job performance review every week.

Mark preached to a group of expressionless, unexcitable parishioners in some churches. Children slept in the back pews, and the adults might as well have been. Following some meetings, listeners emptied the church as if a fire alarm had been pulled.

The aftermath of such services was predictable. Mark returned to our living quarters in a somber mood, quiet and burdened. He cherished the anointed moments when the wind of the Holy Spirit swept across the altar and warmed the hearts of believers. Mark loved praying with people and seeing their needs met, and he was noticeably disappointed when few availed themselves of the opportunity to seek the face of God.

"Mark," I often said, trying to lift his spirits following a service where the people were unresponsive, "that was a wonderful message."

"There were some real needs there tonight, Huldah. I didn't get through to them," Mark said, his head bowed, his body wet with perspiration, his hair looking like he'd just come from a swimming pool.

"You did all you could. You can't force them to the altar."

"I know."

By his heavy sigh it was obvious he was blaming himself, yet there was nothing more I could say to relieve his self-imposed frustration. I invariably went to bed without him, wishing I could tap him on the head with a magic wand and whisk away all his worries. Several hours later, his taxed body crawled under the sheets beside me. His cold feet rubbed against mine, and I knew he had regained the innate optimism I so admired.

I wondered how one man could pray so much, especially after a service that hadn't met his expectations. After conducting early morning prayer meetings at the church, he returned to our apartment to seek God some more. Mark prayed on his knees, while sitting, or while pacing like an expectant father. He lifted his hands and made facial gestures. I had to cackle inside at his unusual gyrations. What a peculiar man I had married, yet there was no one more sincere and dedicated. I knew he often waged spiritual battles far beyond my understanding.

In some ways I thought "Saint Mark"—as I called him—would have been happier living like a monk in a monastery. Many times after services he ate a meal and then found a place to pray and read his Bible alone. And when we traveled together, he often devoted more time to conversing with God than his own wife. After being married for several months, I realized that Mark lived on a different spiritual

plane. At times I even felt inferior. But I learned throughout the years that I had to be myself; I couldn't try to be
Mark Buntain or to attain his level of spiritual intensity.

In my own way I prayed that God would grant us mighty
services. Knowing Mark's apprehension about stepping to
the pulpit until he had an assurance the Holy Spirit would
be by his side, I often directed my prayers to that end. And
seldom was I disappointed.

# 12

# *What Are We Doing Wrong?*

When we accepted the invitation to travel throughout the Northwest District, we became legal residents of the United States. We thereby assumed the rights of U.S. citizens excluding voting privileges. Although we didn't know it, our new status also made Mark eligible for the military draft.

We were in the midst of an eventful nine-week revival in Wenatchee, Washington when Mark received his draft notice. At first, Mark and I were concerned. But when we showed it to Pastor Andrew Teuber, he assured Mark that he would be exempted. The next day Mark went by bus to Spokane, Washington to apply for a clerical exemption.

Our stay in Wenatchee in the spring of 1945 left me with many fond and unforgettable memories. During one of the services, Pastor Teuber told the congregation we liked lemon pie. The following afternoon, church members delivered six pies to our motel room. The people were so courteous, generous, and anxious to see God move.

One night following a service there, a young truck driver asked Mark to ride with him to Spokane on one of his routes. Mark obliged, answering the young man's questions about finding God's will. During that journey God confirmed the driver's calling into the ministry. That truck driver would one day become a well-known evangelist, who, over the years, led hundreds to Christ.

One evening, about 11:00 p.m., we arrived back at our motel room only to see a torrential cloud of smoke hovering over the building. We spotted a room on fire, with flames flickering on the curtain. Mark hurriedly woke the manager and called the fire department. The firemen rescued a man who had fallen asleep while smoking in his room.

Wenatchee became one of our favorite stops, for it was there that we met Ray and Lillian Reems. During the first few nights of the revival, Lillian had played the piano but had not been in the services since. The women in the church had attended the meetings faithfully, many of them picking and packing apples in the orchards all day before coming to church at night. I wondered what had happened when this particular woman was noticeably absent. When we learned Lillian had been stricken with scarlet fever, Mark and I accompanied the pastor to the Reems' ranch to pray for her.

Before the revival was over, Lillian walked through the rear doors of the small chapel completely healed. What a blessing to see God so miraculously answer our prayers.

Following the revival, the Reems invited us to their ranch for a period of recuperation. They owned a large spread of land with their house situated on the pinnacle of a hill—"a mansion over a hilltop." They treated us like royalty, serving feasts at every meal.

As our stay at their resort culminated, Ray handed Mark an envelope containing seven hundred dollars.

"This is to help you buy yourselves a car," Ray explained.

My heart nearly leaped from my chest as Mark lifted the enclosed check to eye level. I peeked over his shoulder to read it for myself.

Tears began gushing from my eyes when I reached to give Ray and Lillian a hug. "Thank you. God bless you. Thank you. Oh thank you," I said, smiling under what had become a waterfall of tears.

When we purchased our first car—a 1939 Plymouth two-seater—we thought we were beginning to climb the evangelistic ladder. After three and one-half eventful months of ministry together, it seemed we were finally off and running.

Some months thereafter, we were reminded of our insignificance. We were scheduled to conduct a series of services at a chapel on the Oregon coast, which, by the appearance of the building's exterior, should have been condemned. We were relegated to the old parsonage adjacent to the church. The dilapidated building had a sink, dresser, an old stove, and a thin mattress barely large enough for two. The cold, damp environment reminded me of the dungeons you read about in history books. The house was an ideal habitat for rats, snakes, and spiders, and the cave-like darkness attracted those fanged, winged creatures seen in horror movies.

That first night I stayed awake, afraid to even close my eyes. I yearned for my decorated room and soft mattress back in Vancouver. Images of home sought to capture my thoughts, as if I had deserted my fortress and now I was about to reap the consequences.

When we had returned to Vancouver weeks earlier, there were no welcome banners stretched across Main Street or parades hailing my return. Home represented something that I valued far more, however: security. During that visit, I didn't let my parents know about the fears that plagued me. I knew it wouldn't do any good to worry them, so I kept my feelings to myself. But this particular evening in Oregon, my emotions rose to the surface with tears.

Mark had learned to live this way. I wasn't sure I could. Moreover, I wasn't sure I could tell him. He was already asleep when my first tear dampened my pillow. That night, just two days before my twenty-first birthday, I cried myself to sleep.

My birthday only compounded my depressed state. But I reached new depths when a well-known evangelist invited Mark and me to his plush hotel for dinner. His clothes were quite expensive, and his sparkling automobile looked like it had just come from the showroom. Someday I hope we can have this type of lifestyle, I wistfully said to myself. Other evangelists were conducting large crusades and reaping financial rewards. Mark, however, received offerings as low as fifteen dollars. "What are we doing wrong? Why aren't we as successful?" I questioned God.

Dad Buntain had advised Mark to be as grateful for ten dollars as he was for ten thousand and to preach the same to ten as he would to ten thousand. That philosophy enabled Mark to overcome temptations of envy, feelings of inferiority, and attacks against his faith. Whenever I became discouraged, he cheerfully proclaimed, "God has everything under control."

Many men could preach about faith, but few practiced it like my husband—even in our early years together. When our love offering was stolen from behind the pulpit during a revival, Mark did not allow it to quench his faith. We were struggling financially at the time, yet Mark believed God would take care of us. And He did.

We understood we had to start at the bottom and that we had to remain faithful despite the difficulties. God had promised to provide what was needed. Still, I wondered if we would ever be financially secure enough to have children and a home we could call our own. Or, would we spend the rest of our lives in decrepit evangelist quarters like this cell in Oregon?

My mind was filled with questions and a trace of envy on my birthday. There was no celebration, no table of gifts, not even a cake. Fortunately, my parents came down for an unexpected visit. Although I was embarrassed for them to see us staying in such a poor apartment, it was glorious to be able to embrace them again.

Despite my pity party and the unfavorable conditions, the meetings in Oregon were successful. Many men and women rededicated their lives to Christ. By the close of the revival the Lord had nestled deeper into *my* heart as well. God was transforming my priorities. I began to recognize the selfishness that had governed my actions and attitudes. Most of all, I now had an assurance that God wanted to accomplish something significant through our lives in spite of our insignificance.

In the months ahead, I realized that being a part of Mark's ministry, although difficult at times, was becoming paramount in my life. I never had felt a specific calling to the evangelistic field; I was convinced, however, that God *had* chosen me to be Mark's wife. And fulfilling that calling was as important as anything. I began seeing each new town and every small church as a new opportunity and challenge, rather than a plight where mere survival was the esteemed prize. I no longer perceived living by faith as a product of God's wrath; it was His way of reminding us that He alone is our daily Provider.

Regardless of my newfound acceptance of our lifestyle, I could never grow accustomed to the rigorous traveling schedule. I deplored the sight of suitcases. Sometimes we had to leave immediately following a Sunday evening service to make it to a new location by Monday evening. There were few chances to catch our breath.

Staying with families in the churches also provided its share of challenges. When work was being done around the house, I felt obligated to help them iron clothes, wash dishes, and can fruit. And no matter what they set on the table for meals, I felt I had to eat it—a lot of it.

Perhaps Mark's greatest qualm was the constant barrage of gossip—often about the pastor—that spewed from the mouths of our hosts. We established a policy never to visit in a family's home unless the pastor had accompanied us or had given prior approval to the dinner engagement.

When we arrived, many of the pastors of smaller congregations were discouraged and needed a fresh touch from God. They had primed themselves and their people for revival. Other pastors saw us as temporary replacements, giving them an opportunity to take a break. One such pastor decided to go hunting for several days during our revival. Mark was noticeably disappointed when he learned of the pastor's departure. I can still remember the perplexed expression that registered in Mark's face.

I said, "Mark, God is still going to be there tonight, and the people are going to be touched. God's presence isn't dependent on the pastor being there." Mark grew thoughtful.

"You're right," he conceded. "You're right."

As the disappointment in his face gradually receded, he leaned over and kissed my forehead and said, "I'm so glad I married you."

That evening several people accepted Christ into their lives, and many others came to the altar to make prayers of rededication. When the service had concluded and we had returned to our room, Mark's face was aglow. It wasn't pride; it wasn't even a slice of revenge that I saw impressed on his smile. It was the sheer pleasure of knowing God had used him to do something significant with a little help from his bride.

# 13
## Wenatchee

Every time we visited their ranch, Ray and Lillian Reems were like our designated guardian angels. They were two of the most giving people we had ever met, lavishing us with an abundance of food and gifts. They had extended to us a standing invitation to visit them whenever we were in the area, so we availed ourselves of their offer as often as we could. Their ranch was a place of refuge where we could regroup and relax without obligations.

While visiting for a few days, Mark and I were awakened before sunrise by a knocking at our bedroom door.

"Mark, it's me, Ray. Can you come out here right away?"

Mark threw on his robe and rushed into the living room. Ray was distraught. A storm was approaching, which by all indications would destroy his cherry crop.

"Mark, can you pray?" Ray asked.

As the ominous storm lowered its ugly head on surrounding properties, Lillian and I watched the two men march into the fields.

Hours later, the storm had passed, and Ray's cherries had been spared. Ranchers and farmers on both sides were hit hard with losses that mounted into the thousands of dollars.

Several years later, we had another frightening experience while staying in Wenatchee. Mark and Ray had left for a fishing trip on Thursday with plans to return on Saturday so Mark could preach the Sunday services for Pastor Teuber. We had prepared a large dinner for their return. As Saturday drew to a close, they still had not arrived. We hadn't even received a phone call.

Because a fierce storm had swept through the region that day, Lillian and I stayed awake like sentries, fearing the worst and pleading that God's protective hand would deliver our husbands if they had encountered danger. The thundering rain on the roof only deepened my concern, convincing me that the weather had something to do with their disappearance. Lightning and thunder shouted from the night sky. The porch shook. The horses shrieked. The chickens flapped their wings against the coop wire like inmates threatening an insurrection.

We called Pastor Teuber, and he had the congregation pray during the morning service. A search and rescue team was gearing up to explore Chelan Lake when the phone finally rang. Lillian's face broke out in a smile when she heard Ray's voice. The water on the lake had become turbulent and had flooded the boat and engine. Mark and Ray had nearly drowned but were able to make it to shore and wait out the storm in a vacated cabin.

When Ray's truck came scuttling up the road at 4:00 p.m. that Sunday, Lillian and I rushed out to greet our two men. Mark's clothes looked like they had been dipped in mud puddles. A shadow-beard was showing through the dirt on his face, and half circles were etched under his eyes.

Two hours later, as if nothing had happened, Mark took the reins of Wenatchee's pulpit to deliver the Sunday evening message. From my pew, I looked at my long-winded husband that night and thanked God he was alive—even though Mark celebrated his homecoming by preaching what seemed like two full-length sermons back to back.

Wenatchee would be the place of another near tragedy in later years. In the middle of the night, Mark woke me and complained of a strange sensation in his face. When I flipped on the light, a monstrous sight stole my breath. Mark's face was swollen grotesquely. His eyes were nearly shut, and his lips were painfully puckered. I quickly called Ray, Lillian, and Pastor Teuber, and they rushed to our motel.

The doctor was baffled at first but eventually traced it to an allergic reaction. The church in Wenatchee was in the process of building a new sanctuary and was meeting in a makeshift tabernacle. We discovered that the pine sawdust, shavings, and straw scattered along the floor had caused the adverse reaction.

Through medication the swelling went down, and soon Mark was able to resume what he so dearly loved: preaching. Ministering from God's Word brought Mark tremendous satisfaction. He lived for it and preached every sermon as if his own life was hanging in the balance. He preached with conviction, knowing lives were teetering on the edge of eternity. The urgency in his voice inspired people to come to the altars. Even though I had heard his sermons quite often, I felt tugs on *my* heart to continue seeking a more intimate relationship with my Savior.

# 14

## *Little Brother Comes On Board*

After eighteen months on the evangelistic field, Mark and I returned to serve as associates under my father. By this time Dad had received an answer to his fervent prayers: the church had moved into a larger facility, which at one time had housed the local YMCA.

My father hoped that when he retired, Mark would replace him as pastor of the thriving congregation. During our six month tenure in Vancouver, the subject surfaced again and again. Each time Mark was unmovable, unwilling to desert God's will even at the expense of comfort and security.

I wanted to stay; Mark knew that. But I wasn't about to make any demands. We hated to displease my father, but when we resigned and left Vancouver, the disappointment on Dad's face was like that of a mourning widower.

Some time later, Fulton, Mark's younger brother, began traveling with us. We attended his graduation from Central Bible College in Springfield, Missouri before setting out for our first series of meetings with him aboard.

On the way to the graduation, our Oldsmobile was beset with flat tires, an overheating radiator, and a dead battery. Nonetheless, we arrived in time to see Fulton accept his diploma. As Fulton strolled across the platform, Mark sat in the audience and beamed like a proud father. Mark knew God had intervened to nudge Fulton toward the ministry. Fulton was pursuing a career in medicine at the University of Toronto when he recommitted his life to Christ and decided to attend Bible college.

Our first revival as a trio was held in a small church in Doty, Washington—nothing like the grandiose rallies Fulton had anticipated. The logging community—like the guest apartment at the rear of the church—was isolated from civilization. Our meetings were incomparable to the large religious rallies held by Charles Price, Kathryn Kuhlman, and Billy Graham that were attracting national media coverage at the time. In fact, reporters from local weekly newspapers weren't even aware of our meetings.

When Fulton crossed the threshold of the apartment, he teased Mark, saying, "So this is the best you can do?"

Fulton was about to begin his indoctrination into the "real" world of evangelistic work.

Mark was extremely conscious of our expenses and only allowed us to eat small lunches. Fulton bemoaned Mark's budget, claiming that his brother was starving us. One afternoon, following a lunch suitable for children, Fulton put a nickel in a slot machine at the entrance of the restaurant. The sudden clatter of coins sounded like someone had dropped a box of silverware. Heads turned from every table.

With his pockets bulging, Fulton grinned and said, "See, Mark, God wanted us to eat more after all."

One Sunday afternoon, as we were conducting a service for a crowded room of inmates, the prison pastor introduced us as Mark and Fulton Buntain and "their wife." Everyone laughed, but I cringed inside and wondered if any inmates there had been incarcerated for bigamy.

Fulton had dated a fine young woman at college; we had gotten acquainted while driving her home after Fulton's graduation. But their relationship was like an on-again-off-again spring shower. While on the road, his blue eyes, blond hair, and charismatic personality attracted many young girls who attended our services. Some females in smaller communities viewed Fulton as their ticket to stardom, excitement, and travel. He even dated some of them. This promptly evoked my motherly counsel: "They're not the right one. Lorraine is the girl for you." She was beautiful, talented, and sensitive. I didn't understand how he could have left her behind.

At a small church in Canada, Fulton learned a valuable lesson when his female distractions led to an embarrassing situation. One snowy day, Fulton went skiing with some girls from the church. Because he was gone all day, we didn't have time to practice our music for the evening service, and I was frantic. That night as we tried to sing "Have You Counted the Cost?", Fulton tried three times to sing his part correctly. Each attempt was more miserable than the last, and his face turned a deeper shade of red with every squeaky note. Thereafter, I had little trouble encouraging him to practice.

At the request of a country minister, we journeyed to a small town in Idaho to inaugurate the establishment of his new church. The larger churches in neighboring communities had pledged to attend and support the meetings, but a blizzard prevented them from blazing through the snow and ice. We had weaved our way through the heavy-falling snow the day before only to discover the man didn't have a church, but that he was hoping to build a congregation from the meetings.

Because of the inclement weather, the meetings had to be cancelled. The bundled-up clergyman came to our room to give us the news, then made a hasty retreat like a God-forsaken man. We watched as he traipsed his way through the snow, facing the inevitability of our departure. Sympathy pangs filled my heart, and I prayed that God would repel the snowstorm with one swipe of His hand so the meetings could be held.

The following morning, we received an invitation to hold a youth meeting at Broadway Tabernacle in Vancouver, British Columbia.

Speaking into the telephone receiver, Mark said, "Pastor, I'm not sure we can come."

"Take it," Fulton coached into his brother's unengaged ear. "Take it."

Mark eventually agreed to accept the invitation, and in no time we were heading over a pass through the mountains. We regretted having to leave, but there was no telling how long it would be before the roads were cleared so the neighboring churches could attend.

As we reached the top of the mountain, cars were at a standstill. A snow slide had trapped about fifteen cars on the summit, including ours. We kept the car running, trying to keep warm while waiting for the snow plow to arrive. All three of us fell asleep.

Within minutes we woke choking in a haze of toxic fumes. Snow had built-up around the muffler. Mark shut off the engine and tried to push open his door, but a snow drift had engulfed it. We were trapped. We grasped our throats in desperation. Moments later, Fulton cracked his door and pried it free with his feet. Coughing uncontrollably, Mark and I stumbled out into a snowfield. We collapsed to our knees, gasping for oxygen.

Then we looked at each other—our clothes wet from the snow—with one of those "Boy, are we stupid" expressions. Despite our carelessness, we were quite grateful for God's protection. Whether we were aware of a precarious situation or quite oblivious to danger during our evangelistic travels, the Shepherd of our souls faithfully preserved us.

# 15

# *Many Questions—
No Doubts*

A week before Christmas, 1949, I learned that precaution-
ary tests were being conducted on my father. He had grown
weak, and doctors were uncertain of the cause. This made
Christmas with the Buntains in Edmonton difficult for me
as my thoughts were tainted with worry.

Mrs. Buntain had prepared a sumptuous feast, and the table
was a work of art with each place setting laid with china
and silverware. Suddenly the front door swung open, and
Dad Buntain led a soiled band of homeless characters to the
dinner table.

By Mrs. Buntain's reaction, these men obviously were not
on her guest list. Somehow their unshaven faces and odorous clothes were incongruent with the beautiful meal she
had crafted. Nevertheless, she graciously made room for her
new guests as if they were members of the family.

A telephone call from my mother bolted me to my feet,
and I excused myself from the table. Mother's simpering
voice announced father's weakening state. Several days later
I boarded a train destined for Vancouver to see my father.

My train was stuck in the snow for forty-eight hours,
including New Year's Eve. Alcohol was flowing freely, and

passengers were dancing. Considering my depressed state, I hated being ambushed with such gaiety. I tried unsuccessfully to block out the laughter, for it seemed so cruel and insensitive.

When I arrived at Deep Cove, where Father was staying, he had lost much of his vitality but was, nonetheless, still jovial. His speech, however, was more deliberate and guarded, and I wondered if he had already determined that his fate was sealed.

Surgery was performed, but afterwards the doctors could offer no promises. Cancer was found in the liver. "We have to wait and see," the doctor said, thereby sentencing us to weeks of uncertainty and worry.

Because Fulton was getting his own speaking invitations and becoming more independent, he set out on his own shortly after Dad's surgery.

It was a sad day for Mark when Fulton boarded the bus for his first solo revival. Mark was happy that Fulton was doing so well, but he knew he would miss him. Mark wasn't just losing a team member; he was losing his best friend.

For miles that day, as we drove past dairy farms, windmills, and large grain bins, Mark didn't say a word. I wasn't sure if he was recounting his childhood memories with Fulton or simply muffling his grief. I just knew the silence had to do with Fulton's departure.

I regretted having to say goodby to Fulton as well. He had become the brother I never had.

We didn't see Fulton much after that, although we did cross paths once at a customs station on the Canadian border. Fulton came running across the road waving to us and shouting, "I got engaged last night! I got engaged!"

"To whom?" I asked.

"Who else?" he said. "Lorraine."

I hugged him and said, "She'll make a wonderful wife. You finally got the right one."

We were holding meetings in Gresham, Oregon when mother called. Between sniffles, she told me the cancer had spread, and Dad was growing worse. Cancer—that obscene word—was threatening to deprive me of my father. My heart felt like it was about to burst; my body wanted to prostrate itself on the floor. Mother's voice took on a whining tone as she conveyed the doctor's prognosis: "He has very little time to live."

That night Mark held me in his lap and let me cry as he affectionately brushed his fingers against my cheek. "God can heal him, honey."

I cried into the waking hours of the morning. Mark arranged for me to catch a train to Vancouver; he stayed to conclude the revival before coming on to Vancouver himself.

Dad was very thin and without words when I arrived at the hospital. The next few days our family prayed constantly that he would be healed. And, in fact, he did mount a recovery. Even the doctors were amazed. At his request, they sent him home.

But, there, at the age of sixty-five, he died with his family at his bedside, without a profound parting phrase or climactic scene. His eyes closed, his breathing became subtle, and his life finally came to an end.

The funeral, conducted by Dad Buntain, was widely attended—a testimony to my father's influence in the community. Throughout the ceremony, images of the past filled my thoughts: the fishing trips, the rides to Bellingham, the heartfelt conversations. Then thoughts of Mother and her future began infiltrating this solemn affair. Where would she go? What would she do?

Mother wept throughout the ceremony but remained brave. I whispered comforting words in her ear—words that weren't even adequate for my own grief. She continued crying. There was nothing else I could say.

When the pall bearers lowered the casket into the ground, I remember how the atmosphere became as black as the ebony-colored dresses encircling the gravesite. The garlands of bright flowers seemed coldly inappropriate at that moment. I despised death, at times trying to reconcile my overwhelming feelings of grief with my understanding of heaven and eternal life.

During the next few weeks, I stayed with Mother. Living with one parent was strange when I had always viewed Mother and Dad as an inseparable pair. I ached knowing that a part of her had been buried in the ground never to walk the earth again.

I never understood why Dad had been taken from us when he had many fruitful years ahead of him. Although that searing question never imperiled my faith in Christ, I must admit it monopolized my thoughts for weeks after he died. And even though I still had not settled on a pacifying answer, I had come to rely on an assurance that God was truly in control.

When Mark asked Mother to travel with us, one would have thought he had sprinkled her with water from the Fountain of Youth. She seemed to have been reborn with excitement. She was a prayer warrior unlike anyone I had ever seen, willing to support our ministry on her knees.

I often wondered what the future held for us. But I knew God had His hand on our lives. That was made real to me one winter night in 1951 in Sunnyvale, California. Suddenly, early in the morning, a rumbling startled us from our pillows. Running outside, we discovered a cyclone had grazed every home on the surrounding streets except the home of the pastor with whom we were staying. The neighborhood looked like foliage from a tree. Homes were in ruin all around us; automobiles were on their sides.

God had once again protected us; and although I did not know what He had in store, I was certain the Lord had preserved us for a special work. I never doubted that, yet occasionally, deep down, I hoped God would give us an assignment where we could hop off the evangelistic ferris wheel and begin a family.

Later that year I went to Auburn so I could help Alice give birth to her third child, Kathy. The baby was so gorgeous. Just being near the infant intensified my motherly impulses.

Mark and I had discussed starting a family on numerous occasions, but I honestly wondered if I would ever have a baby of my own. We knew, ultimately, it was in the hands of the Almighty. So I prayed for heavenly intervention in the months that followed, dreaming and hoping for a special little gift from God.

# 16
## *Separated*

Going to a foreign country to live as a missionary was a frightful thought. Being that far away from my mother was, as far as I was concerned, beyond consideration. I always admired the missionaries who had held services at my father's church; their stories certainly fascinated me but not to the point that I wanted to join them on the field. Growing up, I was always grateful that God had *not* called me to a foreign land.

In Kelso, Washington, we attended a missionary service featuring Howard Osgood, foreign secretary of the Far East for our denomination. He spoke for more than an hour that night enshrining the life of a missionary and declaring the need for evangelists abroad.

Afterward, my fears came true as Mark expressed his interest in overseas evangelism to the guest speaker.

Howard Osgood responded, "Mark, you may be the one we need."

Secretly, I prayed a stint abroad would not materialize.

By the time Mark had officially received an invitation from Reverend Osgood, an elderly farmer in Dad Buntain's church had already offered to pay Mark's airfare. The farmer felt indebted to Mark's father because a cancerous tumor on the side of the man's face had fallen off into a washbasin after Dad Buntain had prayed for him.

Since God had provided the airfare in such a marvelous fashion, I convinced myself that it would be inappropriate to complain. After all, I thought, Mark is deserving of the opportunity. So, outwardly, I appeared excited for him and made plans to stay in Ed and Alice's home in Auburn.

When I waved farewell to Mark at the Seattle airport, my smile crumbled. I returned to Auburn, my face wet with tears, overwhelmed by the emptiness I felt.

Ed had asked me to serve as their Christian education director and office secretary while Mark was away. At first, staying busy kept my mind off Mark. My mornings were spent doing church office work, and the afternoons were devoted to visiting families who hadn't attended Sunday School the previous week. On Saturdays I kept myself occupied by canvassing the neighborhoods. In a short time, the Sunday school attendance increased. After we conducted a vacation Bible school, even more children became regulars.

Despite my active schedule and my hosts' conscientious efforts to make me comfortable, by the third month, I was wishing Mark's trip had never emerged. I missed him terribly. The nights of separation were agonizing—like a newlywed torn from her lover.

During those six months, my desire to have a child intensified, partly because of the loneliness I experienced. We had been married nearly eight years, and I figured it was time we had a baby. I knew it would happen in God's time, but I was convinced *now* was that time.

While Mark was away, Ed drove me to Portland for my driving test. Mark had given me a brief driving lesson, but I was still quite a novice. Although Portland's maze of one-way streets petrified me, I had to take my test there because our car had Oregon plates. Amazingly, the instructor passed me, probably so he wouldn't have to endure the ordeal a second time. I beamed with pride over that temporary license, anxious to show it off to Mark upon his return.

For me, Mark's return rivaled that of Charles Lindbergh. If it had been within my power, there would have been tons of ticker tape thrown from Auburn's windows to celebrate that blessed day. Nevertheless, I was more than satisfied with a long embrace and a lasting kiss.

Mark was exhausted from his trip, having ministered day after day in many countries. His tall frame had dipped to 139 pounds, and his face looked like that of a malnourished refugee. This trip was supposed to get missions out of his system, but it obviously had the opposite effect. All he wanted to talk about was his meetings and the great need for evangelists overseas.

"Huldah, I wish you could have seen it!" Mark exclaimed. "People ran up to be prayed for. When I gave an altar call, they swarmed around me so quickly. It was the most amazing thing I've ever seen. Oh, how I wish you could have been there!"

I had never seen such excitement in Mark. His stories were boundless. I heard the same accounts time and again. One story led into another. He knew he was repeating himself, but he couldn't contain his enthusiasm.

Despite having had his wallet stolen in the Philippines, Mark had brought back a set of Noritake china. Besides my wedding ring, it was the nicest gift anyone had ever given me. Even the china, however, paled in comparison to having my husband home after six months of separation.

# 17

# "I Can't Have the Baby Now!"

"Mrs. Buntain, I have wonderful news. You're pregnant!" the tall gray-haired doctor said.

His words were melodious. God had answered my prayers.

Mark was ecstatic when I conveyed the news. Yet, it was somewhat imposing to think that within nine months we would be traveling the backroads and highways with a child.

In January, 1953, we set out for a tour that took us across Canada to Niagara Falls then down through Michigan into Springfield, Missouri. When we boarded the train, Mother was with us. Our first meeting was in Ontario, Canada, close to where Mark's Aunt Bessie and Uncle Percy lived.

Uncle Percy had been very ill, so it was a timely visit. Although he never had much time for religion, from his sick bed Uncle Percy often listened to Mark preach on the radio. And during our stay, Mark led his uncle to the Lord. A few days later, Uncle Percy died.

Never had I witnessed such an unusual ritual as the wake held for Uncle Percy in his old fashioned farm house. People came in their overalls and stood around his open casket. There was music and singing, a potluck dinner, and one favorite story after another about "good ole" Uncle Percy.

Although we were sad he had left us, it was difficult to be overly mournful. He had suffered many years with a heart condition, and now he was in the presence of the Lord.

Niagara Falls was a memorable sight. The constant, forceful pounding of the water mesmerized me. As we turned to leave, I fell and sprained my ankle. Mark jumped to my aid like a paramedic.

"Are you all right?" he asked, terror in his voice.

"I think so," I said.

He lifted me slowly, concerned not only for my well-being but also for the baby's.

"Shouldn't we get you to a doctor?" Mark asked as I limped from the Falls, unable to put weight on my left ankle.

"I'll be okay." That's what I courageously said; I only hoped it was the truth.

Mark didn't mention his concern for the baby, but I knew that was why he was so insistent about going to the local hospital. Because of God's grace I suffered no repercussions from my "fall at the Falls."

Spending Easter in Springfield, Missouri resurrected some once-conquered obstacles in my life. A famous evangelist was in town pulling his brand new customized trailer behind his silver Cadillac. His wife, meanwhile, was flaunting her fur coat and jewelry.

Again I questioned whether we were doing something wrong. "No," Mark said, "God rewards faithfulness."

There were times, however, when I begrudged our lack of financial security, wondering if God had forgotten to divvy our share of the reward. We were happy, but it seemed like we were having to cope with our share of hardship when other evangelists were enjoying luxury.

When our baby was born several months later, hardship and suffering took on new meaning for me. The doctor had predicted our baby would arrive in late August; therefore

Mark was confident he could fulfill a speaking engagement in North Carolina and be home with time to spare.

During the first eight months of my pregnancy, I had traveled with Mark and found myself the focus of countless jokes from well-meaning pastors. I was relieved to return to Auburn and stay with Alice and Ed in a rented trailer behind their house to await the arrival of our baby—even if Mark was a thousand miles away.

At four o'clock in the morning I woke up in our trailer with severe backaches, unable to get comfortable enough to sleep. Several hours passed, and a series of contractions sounded the alarm. Ed stayed with the children and by that morning, Alice had driven me to Seattle and admitted me into the hospital. All the way to there, I kept repeating, "I can't have the baby now; Mark isn't here yet. I can't have the baby; Mark isn't back."

"He'll be here soon. We'll call him," Alice said. My diaphragm felt like it was going to explode. As the pressure mounted, I thought I would burst at any moment.

Two nurses steered me into the delivery room just before one o'clock in the afternoon. Everything seemed to be progressing as planned until I heard the doctor say something about needing "forceps."

I wanted to leap off the table, but the doctor put his face up to mine and whispered comfortingly, "Everything is all right. You're just fine. We need you to push only when I tell you. Okay?"

I nodded my eyes.

I felt like I was in the middle of a football huddle the way the team of doctors and nurses crowded around me. More and more personnel joined the delivery crew. The sweaty room felt like a steam bath.

Without warning, I sensed tension in their voices, followed by an unnerving commotion. Perspiration drenched my body, leaving my garments soggy-wet.

Before I could object, a nurse stuck a needle into my arm as if it were a pin cushion. Alice, who was by my side, squeezed my hand as I screamed.

The doctor looked me in the eye once more and said, "You're fine, and the baby's fine. It shouldn't be much longer. The contractions caused some bleeding so we're giving you a little blood. Okay? Nothing to worry about."

Minutes later the bleak atmosphere of the room was transformed. Doctors and nurses were smiling beneath their masks and speaking with optimistic inflection in their voices.

A nurse suspended the baby in front of me as if she were presenting a plaque.

The doctor hovered above me, saying, "You did well. You're the mother of a beautiful baby girl."

I wanted to hug the doctor's neck, but the IVs were still in, so I simply slurred, "Thank you; God bless you."

When everyone left the room, I became distressed by Mark's absence. The ecstasy of motherhood had been tarnished by the lonely, suffering moments I had endured during the delivery. "God, why couldn't Mark have been with me for such a special moment? Why couldn't we be together?" I whispered to the ceiling.

I knew he was on his way, but it was a long drive from North Carolina. I suddenly felt the confrontation of emotions that unwed mothers must feel—having to contend with joy and, at the same time, loneliness.

Two days passed before Mark entered my hospital room. He hid his face with a bouquet of flowers and juggled a box of candy in his arms.

As he began to apologize, his voice quivered. Then he closed his eyes and began thanking God for protecting me and blessing us with a lovely daughter.

# 18

## *For Better or For Worse*

Three weeks after our daughter Bonnie was born, we embarked on a hectic traveling itinerary. Many nights were sleepless, and we often had to get off to an early start the next morning. We took our well-behaved baby to the meetings during the day but usually employed a teenager to care for her during the evening services.

To better accommodate a new baby, we purchased a trailer that we could pull from one location to another. That proved to be a costly mistake as far as Mark's physical condition was concerned.

When we arrived in Hayward, California to be with our pastor friends, Jim and Norma Swanson, Mark was suffering from a hernia caused by hoisting the trailer so often. He had to be admitted into the hospital for an operation.

A nurse was about to shave the patient next to Mark, mistaking him for the hernia patient. The man hastily intervened, saying, "That's the first I've heard of removing a guy's tonsils from that end." The room exploded with laughter.

Within a few weeks Mark had recovered and was ready to return to the pulpit. He had been asked to participate in a missionary convention in Medford, Oregon. When we arrived, the pastor regretfully informed us that he had to go away unexpectedly because of a death in his family. So he asked us to take charge in his absence.

When John Hall, veteran missionary to Africa, rose to speak that evening, I didn't realize the impact his words would have on our lives. I could see, however, that something significant was stewing in Mark's mind as Brother Hall shared his piercing message. By the expression on Mark's face, I knew he was weighing every word—asking God if he was being called to a foreign land.

By the time John Hall relinquished the pulpit back to Mark, my husband was wiping his weeping eyes with a handkerchief. I sat, observing, listening with perked ears, and speaking silently to God: I'll do anything You ask, but please don't ask me to take a baby to some hot jungle where there's malaria and other diseases. If You're calling Mark to the mission field, at least wait until Bonnie is a little older.

Mark had long desired to serve as a missionary to China, and I wondered if this convention would encourage him to pursue that option. I didn't know it, but while Mark was in the Orient, he had been offered a full-time position there. At the Tokyo airport, John Clement, missionary to Japan, said, "Mark, why don't you return to this country? Your wife was born here, and you could be such a blessing to us." While Mark pondered the request, God spoke to him in an audible voice, saying, "You will go to India."

We had held revivals in numerous tucked away towns since the missionary convention with John Hall, and Mark had yet to mention anything about wanting to go overseas for an extended period. I was hopeful that God had heard my pleas and had dissuaded him from ministering abroad.

We arrived in Edmonton for a visit, certain Dad Buntain would continue communicating his desire to have one of his sons replace him as pastor of his church. Nothing would have made me happier than being able to raise Bonnie in a comfortable place like Edmonton—anywhere other than the mission field. I knew Mark felt called to evangelistic work, but there was no telling what thoughts were tumbling through his mind.

We had just finished eating breakfast when Mark began sorting through our forwarded mail. He slumped onto the arm of the sofa in his parents' living room, his fingers ripping into an envelope as if he were opening a birthday gift. He skimmed the letter, then handed it to his father. Then it reached my hands. Sent from Maynard Ketchem, Field Director of the Assemblies of God Department of Foreign Missions, the letter requested that we serve as evangelists to India for a year.

Stunned by the news, I translated the meaning of the correspondence in silence. Surely Mark wouldn't take a baby to Calcutta, I kept telling myself.

Mark and Dad Buntain, who had received an honorary doctorate from St. John's University in India, were ecstatic about the news. "Huldah, isn't this wonderful? What an opportunity!" Mark shouted, waving the letter through the air like a flag.

Dad Buntain left the room to relay news of the invitation to his wife.

I said, "Mark, I'll go anywhere, but please don't ask me to take our baby to India."

"Huldah, this is what I've been praying for. I feel this is God's will."

I said sharply, "Do you seriously think God wants us to risk our baby's life by going over to some strange place without adequate medical care? Besides, it wouldn't be fair to take her all over India at such a young age," I pleaded. "It could be dangerous."

"Huldah, it's not that bad."

I couldn't understand why he didn't seem concerned about traveling in India with a small baby. I knew Mark's mind was made up—that he felt God's calling on his heart—

and that pouting, sulking, or crying were useless. Nevertheless, I tried my best to convince him we shouldn't go.

"I'm not going to jeopardize Bonnie's life. Call it foolishness if you want, but in my mind it's just plain old common sense."

Mark threw up his hands, saying, "God will protect us!"

"We can't go, Mark. Bonnie is just too small," I said.

"We're supposed to go," he said. "God wants us there."

Clanging symbols would have been more soothing to my ears than the phrase "supposed to go." How could God send us to this living purgatory? I asked myself.

Mark's parents re-entered the room, so we hastily put a lid on our conversation.

We didn't discuss the issue in depth the remainder of the evening. The next morning, I informed Mark of my change of heart. I would go. The initial shock had worn off, and God had reminded me of my commitment to Mark. I had pledged to take him "for better or for worse."

Mother had returned to Vancouver, so I asked, "What would you think of her going with us? Mother could be a great help."

Mark seemed enthused with the idea.

Encasing my hips in his arms, Mark sang into my ears, "I'll see what I can do. You won't be sorry."

I only prayed he was right.

After informing the foreign missions officials that we would accept the assignment, we met with the Reverend and Mrs. Ovid Dillingham in Lodi, California. They had served as missionaries in India for a number of years and volunteered to share their insights into the culture and lifestyle. That visit invalidated many of my fears concerning food, clothing, water, laundry, and transportation. With their enlightenment, India no longer provoked frightful images of large cobras and packs of lepers.

Mrs. Dillingham said, "Listen, dear, if I can survive four years, you can make it for one."

# 19
## *Calcutta*

August 4, 1954, on Bonnie's first birthday, we flew to New York to meet our ship destined for England. Mother and Mark had visited the "Big Apple" before, but it was my first glance at the Statue of Liberty, the Empire State Building, and other noteworthy attractions. After staying four days in an old Victorian mission house in the Bronx, the four of us boarded the Mauretania, a sleek but massive oceanliner bound for South Hampton.

As the ship drifted from the dock, I remembered the numerous missionaries I had known as a youngster who had sailed from Vancouver to their places of ministry in the Far East. I recalled their poor clothing and their need for money. I wondered if I would be like them when I returned. I had told myself I would never serve as a missionary, yet here I was embarking on an adventure beyond my wildest imagination.

When we arrived in London, we checked into missionary barracks where we were fated to wait three weeks for a passage to India. Our original ship had been cancelled, so everyday we prayed we would find passage on another vessel. The shack-like structure that we inhabited barely shielded us from the thick fog and wind. Mark constantly loaded shillings into a portable heater as if it were a gum machine at a supermarket. We slept layered with clothing and blankets, shivering, our teeth chattering. I wondered if India could be any worse than this.

While waiting for a ship to take us to India, we grew accustomed to the British delicacy of having pork and beans on toast for breakfast. We visited Westminster Abbey, Buckingham Palace, London Bridge, and other attractions using the British rail system. One afternoon, however, the heel of my shoe got caught between the platform and the train. With Bonnie in my arms I was helpless to free myself. Mark was pulling the empty stroller, and Mother's hands were occupied as well. Thinking quickly, Mark was able to grab my arm just before the train sped away, yanking the heel right off my shoe. An hour later, I limped back into the mission barracks wearing my broken shoe and grateful to be breathing.

We finally secured passage to India on the Orangie, a Dutch passenger ship bound for Indonesia. At last we were on our way.

My excitement dulled, however, when I saw that our cabin was a dark cubicle in the hull of the steamliner. I told Mark it stirred up memories of some of the apartments we had inhabited on the evangelistic field.

"It's like they say," Mark laughed, " 'there's first class, second class, third class, and then there's missionary class.' "

It was so warm in our compartment that Mark wasn't beyond putting a self-made window in the wall. Even my hardy mother was complaining, and Bonnie was crying. Needless to say, we spent most of the voyage on deck.

As the waves crashed against the ship, I remembered my journey as a child from Tokyo to Canada. It seemed long ago, and yet the memories were so vivid: the waves, the sun glancing off the ship's smoke stack, the sea gulls circling above like vultures. I had betrayed my youthful vow to avoid the ministry, and now I was about to enter a world that would demand more courage than I thought I could summon. Being on a ship destined for Calcutta wasn't the course I had charted for my life. And even though I knew I was being obedient to God, at the time it wasn't enough consolation. I was petrified.

As our ship passed through the Bay of Biscayne, I thought my life had run its course. We had been warned that we were heading for rough waters; that night it surely felt like we were shooting the rapids on an inner tube. I had suffered with car sickness all my life, but seasickness was far worse. Fortunately, the turbulent seas only lasted a day and night before jello-smooth waters prevailed.

When we entered the Suez Canal, the temperature soared to 120 degrees. Most of the passengers were on deck the entire night in search of relief from the heat. My dress was dripping with perspiration, and my level of tolerance was reaching its limit. We had no such thing as disposable diapers in those days, and that created a nauseating problem of its own. Again I wondered if I could withstand the heat of India.

When the Orangie set anchor off the port of Ceylon, now known as Sri Lanka, we were grateful that missionary Harold Kohl came out on a small boat and boarded our ship. He was a welcomed sight. He assured us we could stay with him and his wife Bea until we were able to catch a ship to Calcutta. Bea was so sympathetic and understanding, willing to listen and give advice.

The first night as their guests I came face to face with a creature crawling above my head in our bedroom. This four-legged, leathery animal had a tail twelve inches in length. I screamed. Mark spilled frantically from the bed to his feet. After sleepily focusing his eyes on the intruder, Mark climbed back into bed. Tugging for his share of the sheet, he said, "You're going to meet plenty of these creatures in the East. They won't harm you. They're your best friends. They eat all the bugs."

I was relieved but still watched the intruder carefully. Finally, I garnered the courage to close my eyes but had difficulty falling asleep. So many thoughts were racing through my mind. I could hardly believe I was on the threshold of doing missionary work.

After a number of days of running from one office to another, we finally booked passage on the City of Madras freighter to Calcutta.

Approaching Calcutta up the narrow and treacherous Hooghly River was like entering the mouth of a dragon. Gusts of warm air blew in my face like the exhaust of an automobile. With each breath I had to swallow the heavy, smoggy particles collecting in my throat. The murky water resembled sewage flowing down a wide gutter, only this current contained dead dogs and cows and even the skeletal remains of a human body. Unclothed natives were bathing in the water. Other villagers congregated on the banks. It made me think of Tom Sawyer and Huckleberry Finn and the Mississippi Queen; then I realized the two settings had nothing in common.

Mark and Mother coughed in unison and covered their mouths with handkerchiefs. I held Bonnie against my breast, wondering if her fragile body could survive the lethal fumes. We were stunned to silence. I could see that even Mark appeared staggered by the dearth of poverty of these scantly-clad villagers. A slight paleness had seized his face.

The ship docked in Calcutta, Thursday, October 6. From the deck we could see a smiling foreigner, who we decided must be our host Dan Marocco. The large, boisterous man had pastored the church in Calcutta for several years.

I reluctantly walked off the ship, knowing each step was one foot closer to my internment in what I deemed a dark, primeval world. Copper-skinned men were chewing and spitting red syrup, which I later learned was *pon*—a leaf comparable to chewing tobacco. I asked a man with Dan

Marocco if they were spitting blood because they had tuberculosis. He laughed and said with his rich Indian voice, "No, Memsahib."

As we shouldered through the crowd, children clamored at our ankles and begged for a coin or scrap of food. So many of them were skinny, puny, and deformed. I longed to gather them in my arms. Their eyes loomed like those of lofty owls, looking at me as if I were a majestic goddess here to deliver them from the cruelties of their world. Tears surfaced in my eyes, thinking to myself that some of the children who had touched me would soon be a bag of lifeless bones.

Dan handed Mark a telegram sent from Mrs. Buntain. As Mark read it, his eyes welled up with tears. Without a word, he handed it to me. It said: "Father ill, cancer, come home at once, one ticket available."

We had left Dad Buntain in good health, so I was flabbergasted at the news. "Are you going to go?" I asked.

"What choice do I have?" Mark said, as I placed my arm around his waist.

After that disheartening news, we discovered that our baggage—clothing, baby food, diapers, crib, and more—had not been unloaded from the Orangie in Ceylon and was now on its way to Indonesia.

On the way to the mission house, Dan described some of the sights we were passing in his jeep, but I wasn't especially tuned in. The cries of the children we had left back at the dock were still ringing in my ears. I felt like a tyrannical empress who had elevated her nose in response to the pervading pleas. Furthermore, my heart was heavy, knowing I would be left in Calcutta without Mark.

The hovels surrounding the waterfront were like youngsters' forts found in the backyards of North American homes: cardboard, wood, plastic, and metal sheets pieced together. There were no calming meadows and timeless streams, no mossy brooks or passive ponds—only a blur of faces in bondage braced against walls matted with filth.

Women in threadbare rags, clutching malnourished babies, froze with venomous glares as our vehicle meandered through the chaotic streets. Two women in particular ignored our Caucasian faces. They were wearing shapely sarees, bracelets, anklets, and toe rings. Jewelry was dangling from their pierced ears and noses. These women seemed displaced, as if they were princesses banished from their palaces. Sharing the street with them were women and children whose wardrobes consisted of nothing more than sackcloth.

I disliked myself for having so much. I wanted to empty my purse into the streets and toss my garments and jewelry into the lap of a disheartened mother so some of them, at least, would have twenty-four hours to live like a queen.

The Marocco's jeep could hardly squeeze down the narrow lanes, and, as we passed, we collected stares from every corner. While Mark and Dan were chatting comfortably, I was incapable of carrying on a conversation. I thought my world had surely come to an end. With Bonnie bouncing on my knee as the ditches in the road jarred our vehicle, I looked at my mother to draw strength. But even she wore a despairing daze.

When we arrived at our dwelling, a two-story home for missionaries, I finally could breathe easier. Although located in a poverty stricken area, the building was fairly nice, nothing like what I had anticipated. There were no rats scampering underfoot, no spider webs draping the windows, and no walls perforated with crude holes. It was tidy and well maintained by an elderly couple who served as the innkeepers. The other missionaries were away at a convention in the hills. Dan and Esther Marocco and their four boys lived in another flat in the heart of the city.

The Maroccos took us to a restaurant on our first night in Calcutta. We had just been served our meal when a man came slithering along the ground like a cobra, sweeping the floor with a worn brush.

"What is he doing?" I protested.

"He's cleaning the floors; he's a sweeper. That's his job; he's in the lowest caste and therefore cannot stand up," Dan explained.

Being totally ignorant of the caste system, I was shocked at this man's degrading position. I wanted the man to stop, to stand to his feet like a human being, but I kept quiet, realizing I had much to learn in this new land.

At four o'clock the next morning, the chorusing spiritual rites of the Muslims awoke the city like the dissonant melody of a rooster on a Kansas farm. My sleeping eyes jolted open at the outset of their loud chanting prayers. The mosque was right next door to our bedroom window. It sounded like howling ghosts had invaded our room. Two hours later, a factory horn sounded outside our window like a train about to crash through our building.

After such interruptions, I couldn't return to sleep and decided to check on Bonnie. I found the face of my fair-skinned daughter covered with soot from the factory. Again I wondered why God had sent us to India where it was difficult enough for an adult to survive, let alone a child.

The sun was at its apex on Saturday of that week when I found myself watching Mark's British airliner lift off the tarmac. An evangelist in Edmonton had raised the money for his airfare, but Mark didn't yet have the funds in hand. After reading the cable and understanding Mark's predicament, a young Christian man at the ticket counter had stamped "compassion" across Mark's ticket and sent him on his way. Mark and I had rejoiced in God's provision, but now I was alone, abandoned in a country where I knew no one other than the Maroccos. I wondered what I had done to deserve this.

Shortly after Mark's departure, Dan invited us to stay in their flat. They were warm Italians who treated us with such kindness. They helped me survive. Mother, Bonnie, and I shared a bedroom. Bonnie, her body baking in this city-wide sauna, made sleeping difficult for us at times. Ounces of perspiration must have dripped from my body that first week.

The electricity frequently faltered, the water was limited, and worst of all, we had no air conditioning. We ran water into tubs and tried to conserve enough to get us through a day. Then the water had to be brought to a boil before even using it for baths. Otherwise, the microscopic organisms would cause one's skin to break into a rash. Even the water from puddles in the streets could cause one's flesh to become red and irritated.

Mother, even though she was uncomfortable, never complained. Meanwhile, I felt my spirits weakening. The humidity was often intolerable, Mark was gone, and we were facing opening night of a well-publicized evangelistic crusade without our featured speaker.

A shamiana—a tent with no sides—had already been pitched on Royd Street, where the church had rented a vacant lot for the services. The meetings had to begin even without Mark.

Desperation had all but set in when I thought of contacting missionary Stanley Shaw in Madras to preach the tent crusade. He accepted our invitation and did a wonderful job. I sang and played the accordion, and Mother played the piano for the large crowds. After a week of well-attended services, I even started a crusade choir.

Despite Mark's absence, many people were coming to Christ at our services, and I was becoming more acclimated to the culture. Shortly after the crusades were underway, Dan received a cable from his mother that his father had died. The following day, Dan boarded an airliner to return to the States for the funeral. When Stan Shaw had to leave, the preaching responsibilities were passed on to Esther. She was an outstanding speaker, but we were both anxious to get our men back.

Because our luggage had not returned from Indonesia, I went to the customs office almost daily to make certain the search was continuing. Finally, we received notification the baggage had arrived, so I immediately went to the customs shed only to find our crates turned upside down and the contents strewn across the ground.

"Take me to the man in charge," I ordered to a clerk in a white uniform.

The young man, noticing my stiff chin, disappeared through a door and returned with his superior. I tried to be firm, but my backbone turned to jelly and my face fell into tears.

"What are you crying for, ma'am?" the man asked sympathetically.

"My baby has been without diapers and baby food, and now my crates are turned upside down in the back."

The man patted my shoulder and ordered his men to restore the contents to the crates immediately. My faith was strengthened that day as I saw God's intervention in the situation. My sense of humor also returned as the "coolies" pondered over the dozens of white pieces of cloth called diapers—luxuries their babies did without.

From the Marocco's veranda I watched monkeys trapeze through the trees across the street. One day, however, more than animals caught my eye. The moon's phosphorescent glow provided enough light to see a man obviously suffering with leprosy leaning against a gate to a large manor. I wanted to cross the street to talk to him, but just as soon as my courage peeked a black Rolls Royce streamed out the gate past the shouting beggar. How pitiful, I thought, this man had no hope. He is despised by everyone. He is unclean. Yet, when Jesus was alive He thought nothing of touching lepers.

The man's hands were sunken in his sleeves, and his face was shadowed by a monk-like hood and scarf. Only the bridge of his nose and his dark, sullen eyes were visible. It looked like he was wearing three layers of rags.

Just before the darkness had engulfed him, pye dogs, their tongues exposed, came to his side. Suddenly images of Job and the story of Lazarus and the rich man came to my mind.

The Maroccos later explained that some beggars rented babies as props in hopes of increasing their take from sympathetic Westerners. For some, begging was a lucrative profession. But this leper was different, I decided. He was an outcast, deemed the disgrace of a nation, fit only for a leprosarium. To the superstitious of Calcutta, his soul had been damned by the gods—and no "clean" man would dare be his friend.

That particular indigent man re-entered my view as I spied out the window again and again. I could only bow my head and pray for him, knowing that Jesus loved him and so did I.

# 20
## *Protected*

I nearly tackled Mark—like a teenager mobbing her idol—when we were reunited in Calcutta's air terminal. His father was still ill, but everyone had agreed Mark should return to his work in India. For me the separation had been like six grueling weeks of a survival training course.

The services in the tent on Royd Street continued, but soon we realized we needed a more permanent structure. The monsoon rains and hottest season would soon be upon us. Besides, the tent was already overcrowded. Dan and Mark attempted to negotiate the purchase of the Royd Street property where they could construct a building, but the owner refused to sell. Finally, after weeks of investigation and searching, they located a hall above a nightclub on Park Street.

Soon after the meetings had moved to the new location, we bid farewell to the Maroccos and left to conduct a tent crusade in Jamshedpur, an overnight's journey from Calcutta.

The meetings in Jamshedpur had been effective with many coming forward to receive prayer and accept Christ. But one night, something more than the Holy Spirit swept in. Mother and I had just finished singing and stepped into the audience to find a seat. We normally sat on the platform the entire service, but that night we felt compelled to sit elsewhere. Suddenly, a thunderous explosion reverberated in the atmosphere. Hurricane-like rains and winds came from nowhere. The tent swayed and flapped like a massive kite. Then the posts buckled, and the tarpaulin collapsed onto the listeners.

Mark commanded the people to be calm while I crawled to the main power box to turn off the electricity. Despite Mark's instructions, people were screaming hysterically in the darkness. Moments later the tent was pulled back, and they were able to free themselves. Mother and I then inspected the platform for damages to the equipment. The two chairs we normally occupied were creased by a large support beam that had fallen during the uprising. We looked at one another knowing God had spared us, and for that matter, He had protected the entire audience. Only two villagers experienced minor lacerations.

In the middle of a subsequent crusade in Jamshedpur, God preserved Bonnie's life. One morning at about five o'clock, Bonnie, who was not yet two years old, escaped her crib and crawled out of our bungalow into a courtyard. She climbed up a spiral staircase to the terrace. That night Mark dreamed Bonnie was up on a high building about to fall; instantly, he awakened and saw her crib empty. By following her weeping voice, Mark was able to come to her rescue.

We returned from Jamshedpur just in time for the Puja Celebration in Calcutta. The city was closed down for more than a week for this religious Hindu festival. I had never seen so many parades, costumes, large ceramic idols, and people dancing in the streets. Drums beat constantly until my ears heard noises when there weren't any noises. Along the Hooghly River—a tributary to the Ganges—natives tossed burning pots of live coals and idols into the water as an offering to one of the thousands of Hindu gods they worship. The Indian people spend thousands of rupees on their offerings and costumes, saving money the entire year for the event.

The Maroccos then took me to the Kali Temple. We walked through an eerie, dark passageway lined with persons begging for money. Inside, people were bowing before the clay image of Kali—the goddess of destruction—as if she were almighty. Its charcoal exterior was highlighted by a bright red tongue and layers of necklaces and bracelets.

Suddenly, many of the worshipers rose to leave. We followed them out into the quad area where we witnessed a young goat being pulled into a stall. A man, I figured to be a priest, raised a machete above the animal's neck. I wanted to run to its rescue and free the animal. But the sword sliced through its flesh with one swipe. I turned my head away in disbelief, feeling as though I could vomit.

Some weeks later, Dan Marocco picked up his morning newspaper and read the headline: *Night Mail Crashes, All on Board Dead*. The night mail were inexpensive midnight flights originating in Calcutta, Madras, and Delhi—all destined for Nagpur. Mark was on the flight from Calcutta to Nagpur, so at first glance Dan feared the unthinkable. He read the article that morning before coming to my room. "Huldah," he said as he knocked on the door.

"What is it?" I asked, noting a peculiar expression on his round face.

"Listen," he said, "Mark's all right. He wasn't on board the flight that crashed last night."

"What crash?" I asked.

"The Night Mail. Mark got off in Nagpur to go to Madras, and the plane crashed as it left Nagpur for Delhi."

A nauseous feeling came over me knowing he could have been killed.

I asked, "There weren't any survivors?"

Dan shook his head. "No. Mark was the only passenger who got off the plane to go to Madras."

He handed me the newspaper. As I read the account, I thought of all the people I had seen board the flight that night—people who had now entered into eternity. A small Indian boy. A family. A grandmother.

I wanted to cry, but I couldn't. I was sorrowful for those who had lost loved ones, yet grateful that God had arranged for Mark's safety. In the weeks and months that followed I would repeat that prayer of thanksgiving for God's protection—especially for Bonnie.

Soon we set out for a tour to South India, which is known for its blistering heat and spicy-hot food served on banana leaves. Almost everywhere we went, villagers reached to touch our white skin and pinch Bonnie's cheeks. Her face was bruised by their inquisitive fingers.

Adjusting to Indian culture took its toll on our little daughter. Because we had to wash her diapers in a washbasin with potent South Indian soap, her sensitive skin broke out in a painful rash. Along the way she also developed a cough that turned into bronchitis. We put Vicks into boiling water to serve as a vaporizer, and Mark and I took shifts keeping an eye on her crib. She often coughed throughout the night.

Together we prayed one evening and instantly, steadily, she began to improve. Bonnie's condition had given us a scare, and we hoped we had seen the worst of these fretful, health-related episodes. Little did we know what the enemy had waiting for us.

# 21

## "I Have Finished the Course"

It was a warm afternoon, ideal for sitting around a swimming pool or reading a book beside the ocean. But such pleasantries would be hard to find in this sun-dominated city. Every pore of my body perspired as I labored to remove the particles of dust that seemed to invisibly parachute onto our furniture and floor. The filthy, soot-like air made housecleaning a daily ritual in the Marocco's flat. My sweating feet sunk into my shoes as if I were wearing sponges. Because of the beating heat, sleeveless dresses were a necessity.

This particular day, however, my closet was nearly empty and my hamper overflowed with sun-reeking skirts and dresses that were in need of soap. Loading clothes in the old Maytag was a continual chore. We prayed constantly for the rattling machine and wondered how long it would last.

The wrist-length sleeves of my cotton dress were rolled above my elbows as I swept a mound of dirt into the hallway. These were the odorous kinds of days when my heart yearned for the cool breezes of the Pacific and the lazy days of summer at my parents' cabin.

Our one-year term had seemed like an eternity. Although I had grown to love the people of Calcutta, visions of my homeland were luring me from them: running water, restaurants, television, family, cold drinks, shopping centers, and swimming pools. Mark, on the other hand, had expressed his regret about leaving India. He could only think of the diseased, the homeless, the hungry, the elderly, and the illiterate. I was concerned about them, too. Even though we had helped so many, the task of rejuvenating the teeming masses seemed overwhelming and impossible.

While I was cleaning our flat one evening and Mark was studying on the veranda, the phone rang. He left his Bible open and lunged for the receiver.

As he listened, he became somber.

Mark's firm voice was quivering. "I love you, Mom. Remember, God has everything under control."

The telephone conversation had concluded, but Mark was still grasping the receiver. He sat motionless for a few moments and stared across the room.

"Is there anything wrong?" I asked.

"It's Dad; he's taken a turn for the worse."

Every day Mark had knelt in prayer for his father's healing. Our church had held special prayer meetings, and we had received letters from supportive friends around the world. An abundance of faith had bombarded heaven on his behalf. But now, by his mother's own admission, Mark's father was nearing the end of a prestigious ministerial career. Consequently, we began making plans to return to Canada sooner than we had expected.

On the flight back to Edmonton to see Mark's father, Bonnie swallowed a Lifesaver whole. She began gasping for air as the candy lodged in her narrow windpipe. I tried hitting her back and rubbing her throat—to no avail. Mark reached his finger into her mouth and still couldn't dislodge it. By this time the stewardesses and passengers had been aroused. The hole in the middle of the mint allowed Bonnie to get some oxygen, but the two-year-old was in a panic.

A tall, slender stewardess, thinking quickly, took Bonnie and hung her upside down. When the Lifesaver eventually popped onto the carpet, all the passengers joined us in congratulating the young lady for a job well done.

Mark's mother and Bob Tatinger, the associate pastor at Dad Buntain's church, met us at the airport. Mark and his mother embraced and wept together for a few seconds before she awarded Bonnie and me with an affectionate squeeze.

We went straight to the hospital. Dad Buntain welcomed us as we entered the room and even beckoned us closer so he could give us a hug and get a good look at Bonnie. The pancreatic cancer had rendered him weak and thin. His hair was sprinkled with gray. It was hard to believe here laid the man who had served in the highest office of his denomination, the man who had built a church from eighty to one thousand members, the man who had started a Bible college.

Mark and his mother found it difficult to stay in the room with him after he slipped into a coma, so I sat beside his bed each day while others held a prayer meeting in the lobby. The Sunday night before his passing, when everyone had gone to church, he bolted up from his bed and said, "Huldah!"

I nearly fell off my chair in disbelief. "Yes," I stuttered, wondering if God had performed a supernatural healing in response to the myriad of prayers.

"Get me a pencil and some paper. I have to finish my book on the Holy Spirit."

I obliged his request by holding a paper for him, but he scribbled a few words then fell back onto his pillow.

The day before his death, he rallied again. Mark, his mother, Bob Tatinger, and I were there. The church statesman opened his eyes halfway and said, smiling, "I have fought the good fight; I have finished the course." Then his eyelids gradually shut, and he lost consciousness.

The following day, with Mark, Bob, and me by his side, Dad Buntain went to be with the Lord.

Bob turned to Mark and said, "Now it's all yours."

Knowing he was referring to the church, college, and radio ministry, Mark shook his head and responded, "No, my calling is India. Bob, God has called you to continue this work."

Although Mark's response caught me off guard, I didn't give it much credence. I said to myself, "Surely he doesn't mean we'll be returning *soon* even if he is serious."

We immediately left the hospital to tell Mrs. Buntain of her husband's passing. As we road to her home, I tried to determine what could be said to Mark to console him, but every cliche seemed inadequate. Silence reigned.

Mark threw his arms around his mother, and together tears gushed down their cheeks. As they wept into each other's hair, their chins vibrated without words.

# 22
# *Send Someone Else*

After Dad Buntain's funeral in 1956, Bonnie and I stayed with Mark's mother for six weeks. Some nights I listened outside her bedroom door as she tried to mute her crying. She often cradled her husband's robe or pillow and sobbed. Everything in Edmonton reminded her of him. The memories were inescapable. Dad Buntain woke at four o'clock every morning and fried himself herring for breakfast. The peculiar smell that she had detested no longer lingered in the house. Now she missed it dearly.

Mrs. Buntain's weeks of mourning had dissolved and my broken ribs, suffered from a fall down some stairs, were beginning to heal when I arranged a rendezvous with Mark in Yakima, Washington, where he was holding a meeting. My reunion with Mark elated me, but the joy of the moment was short lived.

Mark said, "I just received a call from the Assemblies of God headquarters, and they want us to return to Calcutta as soon as possible."

I felt the rhythm of my heartbeat change. My nose must have curled, and I know my eyes squinted.

"So what did you tell them?" I asked.

"I told them we would go as soon as possible."

"You told me it would be for one year, and that would be it," I argued, trying to repel the darkness that was clouding my thoughts.

"I know, but that's where God wants us."

I bit my bottom lip. God hadn't called me to India in the first place. I went because I was committed to Mark—God had called me to be his wife. I loved the people in India and did want to help them, but I felt we had already done our part. Why couldn't Mark and I just enjoy a normal life for once and serve one of the large churches that wanted us as their pastors?

Bonnie suddenly waddled into our conversation. "Mommy, why are you crying?"

I lifted her well above my head and drew her cheek to my lips. "It's nothing, go on and play," I said with a cosmetic smile.

As she left the room, I pointed to her backside. "You want that innocent child to grow up in another country? You say we're going back for one more year. I know you. We may never come back!"

"Think of all the people we can help," Mark said passionately. "Calcutta needs us more than ever. The Maroccos are going to be leaving."

"I know, but we're not the only ones in the world who can replace them. Why can't someone else go over, someone who doesn't have a child?"

"I understand your concerns and worries. I do. All I know is that God wants us there. He'll take care of Bonnie," Mark sighed, then, in a softer tone, he asked, "Will you at least pray about it?"

I couldn't bring myself to argue any further. I threw on my coat and scarf and walked out into the snow, trying to deal with my resentment and fear. I needed to hear from God myself.

An hour later, my eyes red with tears, I returned to the house and said, "Mark, I'm going to go back with you because I'm your wife and I love you. I'm not overjoyed with the idea, but I know when you've heard from God. I can't question that."

Before I could say another word, he cupped my jaw in his hand and said, "I understand. So does God, and I know He's pleased by your sacrifice."

Outside, the snow softly sifted from the sky. Inside, my tears poured even more rapidly as I dwelt on my love for God and Mark and the nightmare of returning to Calcutta.

Even though I had made the concession to go overseas, it was weeks before I could bring myself to believe it. The thought of spending the rest of my life amidst the gloom and poverty of that needy city depressed me. A lifetime in Calcutta was more than I wanted to comprehend.

Prior to our departure, we visited Ed and Alice in Walla Walla, Washington, where they were now pastoring. While Alice and I leisurely walked throughout their neighborhood one afternoon, I let my tears flow unabashedly as I shared my concerns.

Alice understood the tormenting fears a woman in my predicament faced. The prospect of going to Calcutta for an extended period would take away any hope I had for a normal family life. We both knew that once Mark got involved in the work there, it would be difficult for him to leave India.

Knowing Mother did not have the financial means to return with us only added to my distress. Nevertheless, my mother advised me to support Mark and be loyal to what God had called him to accomplish. I would miss her. She had shared the load of missionary and household responsibilities in India, but it was her emotional support I would miss most.

Up until a week before we were to leave, I prayed that God would supply the funds to pay Mother's fare. I told the Almighty I needed her more than ever. Then, during dinner one night at Beulah's house, some dear friends pledged to send Mother back with us.

When I heard the news and crawled into bed that night, it was as if I knew God had heard my prayers and was saying, "You see, Huldah, I'm with you. I'll never leave you, nor forsake you."

# 23
## *Tempted to Return*

When the hatch of the prop airplane swung open, heat and humidity swept in like wind off the Sahara desert. The Calcutta air nearly sent me sprawling back into my seat. Temptations to stay aboard for a round trip flight back to the States appealed to my flesh. But when I rose from my seat, I knew there was no escaping it. Calcutta would be my home—until God told Mark otherwise.

The mission house had closed by this time, so we stayed with the Maroccos in their flat. An evangelist was holding meetings for them at the time, so twelve of us occupied their small, modest apartment for several weeks.

Our first night in Calcutta I didn't sleep. I had forgotten how hot it could be, and the small fan at our feet only blew hot air. I hopped out of bed in hope of finding some relief on the veranda. There I thought about the long perspiring work days ahead of us. Since we had left, the church had been beset by internal squabbles and other fiscal problems. The church still met in the upstairs hall, but a strong faction of members wanted to become independent of the Assemblies of God and did not want to affiliate with any particular denomination.

In August 1956, the Maroccos boarded a boat for America. As I watched them leave Indian soil, I knew the load would now rest on our shoulders.

Every night for weeks, Mark met with the deacon board, trying to resolve the differences and establish a fresh direction for the church. Several board members who resented Mark's Western ideas opposed his every compromise and solution.

In the small hours of the morning, Mark returned from these meetings enraged, disappointed, and worried. He often paced the floor and prayed all night until the Muslims began chanting at dawn.

Some evenings, with the air filled with the crooning of Calcutta's insects, I heard Mark's slowly planted feet climbing the stairs to our flat. I met him at the door, waiting up so he could report the outcome of the meetings and release some of the emotional tension. For him, it was just another spiritual battle requiring fasting, perseverance, and prayer.

Night after night as Mark relayed the problems and his frustrations, I felt my righteous indignation rising. I asked God why we had to come to this place where, for so many years, the Protestant churches had not flourished. In some ways, the strife was more grueling for me because I could only watch the confrontations from the sidelines. I wasn't a participant. I was like the trainer who kept her husband mentally and spiritually fit for the verbal artillery that he faced. There were nights when I didn't sleep well because of the hostilities foaming inside me. My deflated pillow was anything but a resting place; it had become a launching pad for my vengeful thoughts. In these moments of weakness, I had visions of telling Mark it was not worth it and we should go home to greener pastures.

In these turbulent days, I often found refuge in the knowledge that the church was experiencing unprecedented growth. The years of work of Dan and Esther Marocco and the hours Mark and I had spent walking through the city, into slum areas, contacting visitors and children in our Sunday school, were finally paying off.

The upstairs hall—where I sang and Mark preached every night—continued to be crowded. Rambunctious patrons in the nightclub below fought for the attention of the parishioners. Our church members could hear colliding bottles and loud dancing through the tiles. So Mark proposed to the deacons that the church again seek to purchase property and build a new facility. Immediately, he was confronted with resistance and demands that the church become independent of the Assemblies of God.

Field Director Maynard Ketcham arrived in Calcutta one afternoon to review the situation in our area and make recommendations to the international headquarters. He knew the struggles that we had encountered.

Labeling the city as "one of the most difficult mission fields in the world," he said, "I know you're disappointed, and I wouldn't blame you if you want to leave. If that's what you want, I'll give you your airfare right now so you can go home." He shook his head and added, "Nothing has seemed to work here in fifty years."

Evangelists had passed through and told us we were fools to bury ourselves in a foreign country when we could have a successful ministry in North America. With that thought in mind I was tempted to stick out my hand for the return airfare, when Mark suddenly spoke up: "No, I believe God sent us here."

"Listen, Mark," the man said, "if you feel a call to missionary work, there are other countries we can send you to. You've proven your abilities."

Mark was a prize fighter who preferred being knocked out to throwing in the towel. And even though I didn't want to leave under duress or a cloud of failure, part of me wanted to go *anywhere* else.

"Just give me a little more time," Mark bargained with Brother Ketcham.

The representative agreed.

In the weeks that followed, we had to cope with a barrage of criticism spewing from the lips of several leaders in the church. Bitterness began seeping into my heart, and, at first, I found myself doing nothing to prevent its occupation. Realizing that was wrong, I sought God's forgiveness. Soon, with the Lord's help, all bitterness bled from me. I knew these obstinate few needed prayer—only God could change their hearts. So, faithfully, Mark and I went to our knees until our Lord gave us direction.

Mark called a special meeting for the church membership to confront many of the issues that had divided the church. He stood behind the podium and rendered one of the most powerful messages I ever heard him make. From the front row I wanted to applaud.

"I'm Assemblies of God, this church is Assemblies of God, and we plan to build an Assemblies of God church," Mark said. "If you don't want that, there are other churches you can attend. Those not wanting to be with the Assemblies of God, stay seated; everyone else stand. Those seated may now leave."

Everyone stood in support of Mark's proposal. God wrought a tremendous change of heart. The board, thereafter, graciously accepted his plans and leadership.

That night, as it fell toward morning, Mark and I basked in apparent victory, unaware that the battle had just begun.

# 24
## Mark's Dream

Mark and I never considered ourselves thrill seekers, but we enjoyed riding a motor scooter—our only form of transportation in those early days. I hopped on the back of the scooter, and with Mark manning the gears, we cruised through Calcutta's traffic. As the wind dried the perspiration from our faces, we enjoyed this temporary escape from the horrors around us. We especially liked to ride along the Hooghly River and watch the ships on their way to port.

But this simple pleasure nearly ended in disaster when Mark, while riding alone, was hit by a taxi. His two-hundred-pound frame catapulted over the hood of the car onto the pavement in an intersection. The bone-crunching fall badly bruised his shoulder and arm.

After that, we decided it was perhaps the appropriate time to request a car from the Assemblies of God. Within a few months we were able to purchase a vehicle that was used for errands and as a Sunday school bus. Mark felt a little safer in a car, although I wasn't sure any North American could avoid feeling vulnerable in Calcutta's maze of traffic.

It was a typical light-lunch afternoon, and the heat was spreading my butter onto my bread roll. I had just taken my first savory bite when a woman from our church landed at our door. Her sister had died, and she said she needed my help. Little did I know I was about to be initiated into the mortician profession. She asked me to help her scrub and dress the body. I turned as cold as the cadaver with fear, but I didn't let the woman know that I was shaking inside.

By the time I entered the door of our flat that evening, the queasiness had worn off. Mark's face, on the other hand, looked almost like that of a corpse. I knew something was bothering him.

"What's wrong?" I asked.

"The owner of the Royd Street property turned us down again to buy his land."

"Surely there's other property, Mark."

"Where? We've been looking for weeks."

Leasable, undeveloped real estate was almost non-existent. Calcutta was a cramped city void of vacant lots, especially near the Royd Street area. Even though he was convinced God intended to give us land, Mark was growing discouraged and tired. I felt his frustration as well, just knowing the diligence with which he had sought to obtain the Royd Street property. Mark's dream was to build the first church of its kind in more than a century.

We continued to comb the city, investigating slivers of useless land. No property appeared suitable for our growing congregation.

Mark, meanwhile, pleaded persistently with the Royd Street owner to sell. Constantly the man rejected the proposals without explanation. We assumed he had received criticism from the Muslim community for renting the plot of land—where Dan Marocco had pitched his tent—to Christians.

After weeks of stalled negotiations and finding himself in a desperate predicament, the owner finally agreed to sell us the property if Mark could only help him rectify his tax problems.

Mark sensed God at work. Every afternoon for weeks, he sought sessions with government officials trying to locate someone, anyone, who could untangle the tax dilemma that plagued this Muslim. Mark was more than persistent—he was driven. But more often than not, he returned home distraught, weary of having his pleas ignored.

I was battling the frustrating conditions myself. The heat and humidity were so high that the tar was running off the streets into the gutters. Kleenex were fastened to my wrists with rubber bands to keep the perspiration off my accounting books and the personal letters I wrote in response to donors. Seeing Mark face disappointment day after day just added to my turmoil.

An attempt to see the proper magistrates one afternoon ended for Mark like all the rest, but as he was leaving the tax building a young man summoned him into his office. The man shared with Mark how his wife had been healed of tuberculosis during one of our tent meetings on Royd Street, and having heard of our predicament, he pledged his assistance in the matter. Thus, he began the lengthy process of clearing the liens so the real estate could be sold to the church.

Before the legal dispute was completely settled and we had raised the funds necessary to build the church, Mark, in faith, scheduled a ground breaking ceremony. But as that momentous day of celebration approached and numerous religious dignitaries were scheduled to arrive, I contemplated how embarrassing it would be if we were unable register the land to build the church. What would happen if the tax problems were never resolved? What if we couldn't raise enough money?

Mark held prayer marathons and fasted entire days. Meanwhile, I worried enough for the two of us. Then one afternoon God reminded us of His presence—that He was marching before us to defeat the enemy's schemes. The land was finally registered, and, shortly thereafter, a cable arrived with word that the church had received a $20,000 donation to begin construction on a building.

Mark and I wept and laughed that day, repeatedly thanking God for His blessings. At the time, however, we didn't realize just how blessed we were. A few days later, a British contractor agreed to build the entire church for $20,000, even though material costs alone would exceed that amount.

Days after construction was to begin, we once again found ourselves on our knees before God. The church property had at one time been swampland, and the ground was too moist for the contractor to lay the foundation. Excavation had come to a halt. In order to build, the engineer would need to drive large beams beneath the earth. The price for such a maneuver was too expensive for the church to even consider.

From the corner of the yard one tropical morning, I watched Mark drive a shovel into the muddy ground. He shook his head in disgust, picked up a handful of dirt, and splattered it to the ground. Then he walked past me like a little leaguer who had just heard "strike three" called with the bases loaded.

Nothing I said to Mark could lighten the burden he was carrying. I knew the importance of this project to his credibility as a leader. To the congregation, Mark was a minor Moses, the man chosen by God to usher in a new beginning for Christianity in this needy city. He couldn't fail. In a strange way this was his Red Sea, the ultimate challenge.

On a Wednesday morning in 1959, with a backdrop of soaring towers left over from the British occupation, Mark and I stood on the property and joined hands with our parishioners. There we lifted our heads in prayer, waiting on our heavenly Father to complete the miracle He had started. I couldn't believe our Lord would allow the project to progress to this stage just for it to fail. I hoped this was merely a mote in need of a drawbridge. An imaginary list of donors ran through my mind, wondering who could be approached about paying to have the beams installed.

Mark, meanwhile, resorted to prayer and more prayer. The next few days, in the midst of this setback, Mark tucked himself away in a dark room to be alone with God.

Friday came, and we still were without a solution; no donor had stepped forward to underwrite the additional costs. Sunday evening the congregation prayed for a miracle. Tuesday rolled around, and still no answer came.

But forty-eight hours later, on a starlit night, Mark and I sat down to our first candlelight dinner in a great while. We were celebrating the watchful eye of God and the miracle of a generous contractor who had decided to implant the beams at his own expense.

As the grand opening of the newly constructed church approached, Mother received some disheartening news. My grandmother was seriously ill, and it was necessary for Mother to go to her bedside. Mother had worked and prayed so faithfully; it was regrettable she had to miss the church dedication. Three months after she returned to Vancouver, Mother cabled me that my grandmother had passed away.

December 1959, the new church opened and held its first service. Mark and I were like children on that special Sunday as we studied the new chapel and admired what God had built.

It soon became apparent, despite the church's beauty, that the building wasn't complete. Most denominations in Calcutta already had their own church-run schools. As parents joined our church, they came expecting us to educate their children like other churches had in Calcutta since the early 1900s. It was essential, we learned, that we provide basic education not only for the children of our parishioners but other children as well. Thus, we made plans to leave on furlough so we could raise funds in America and Canada to build a school.

The Assemblies of God sent Jim and Velma Long and their three children to serve as our replacements while we were stateside.

On our way home from meeting the Longs at the airport, our station wagon broke down with a flat tire. To the waifs living in the neighboring huts, the sight of the blond-haired, blue-eyed Long family was like having a traveling circus break down in front of one's house. Unclothed, dark, copper-skinned children swarmed around the car to get a closer look at this Caucasian family with sun-burned faces.

Jim Jr., the Long's eight-year-old, had his face pinched and his hair pulled by the Indians. The frightened youth couldn't defend himself because he was trying to protect the family's luggage, which had also attracted the attention of the Indian children.

This was a rude initiation to the culture, especially for their children, but the Longs were fine, dedicated people. We were confident they would adapt quickly to their new environment.

Our one-year term in Calcutta had become a six-year stint, but I wasn't complaining. A new church had been built, the congregation had multiplied, and plans had been drawn to build a new school. If we hadn't needed to raise funds for an education facility, Mark would have been content to stay in Calcutta and forgo our furlough. And if I had known what the next twelve months would unveil, I too would have gladly stayed behind.

# 25
## "Why Me?"

I was about seven months pregnant when we left Calcutta on furlough. Before returning to Springfield, Missouri, we stopped to do some sightseeing in Beirut, Amsterdam, Rome, Zurich, and Jerusalem. Physically, I wasn't up to taking in all the tours, so I encouraged Mark and Bonnie to go each day without me.

As I sat alone in our hotel room in Jerusalem, admiring the windswept sky and the architecture unique to the Holy City, I dared to speculate that my illness was more serious than just morning sickness. Not wanting to disrupt Mark's vacation, I refrained from telling him.

Hours before we landed in Springfield, I could conceal the extent of my sickness no more. "Mark," I said, "something's wrong."

His expression became serious. "What's wrong?"

"I'm just worried about the baby. I've been feeling sicker these past few days, and my mouth is full of sores."

Mark pulled a blanket from the overhead compartment and covered me, then laid his hand on me and prayed.

I shut my eyes, trying to block out the horrifying image of a lifeless child in my womb.

Mark canceled his plans to speak to the Assemblies of God officials in Springfield, and within several days we flew to Los Angeles so I could be examined by a gynecologist Alice had recommended.

The following week I succumbed to a combination of nausea, depression, and self-pity.

The world became glorious and happy again, however, when the female doctor announced my baby was all right. Even so, she warned me to be extra careful since this was an unusual pregnancy.

We drove to Vancouver then on to Kamloops for a family outing. Although I still felt weak and nauseous, the doctor's report had put an end to my worries.

Beulah and her family, as well as Mother, had joined us at a spacious cabin overlooking a scenic lake. Everything was conducive to relaxation and recuperation. Nonetheless, without warning, I was suddenly overcome by whatever ailed me.

Mark rushed me to a local doctor who advised me to see the specialist in Los Angeles as soon as possible. "Something is seriously wrong," he said.

The drive to Los Angeles was a merry-go-round of stress and fear, grappling with the spiritual question of suffering and pain and the unknown condition of the baby inside me. Why would God allow me to endure such hardship when I had done so much for Him?

My burning questions intensified when, before I even met with the specialist, Mark had to be admitted to the hospital for a second hernia operation. "Why, God, are You allowing this to happen to us?" I asked time and again. "Have we disobeyed You? Are we out of Your will?" I couldn't understand why, after all our years of service and sacrifice, this was happening.

Fulton was pastoring in Long Beach, California at the time, so with Mark in the hospital, Lorraine volunteered to take me to the specialist.

When the technician maneuvered the X-ray machine into position, I felt like this entire experience was happening to someone else. I knew something was wrong, but I didn't want to admit it to myself.

I waited for the doctor to read her findings. She entered typically, holding a clipboard and a stethoscope. "I'm sorry, Mrs. Buntain. The baby is dead," she said with the empathy of a mother.

The word *dead* echoed in my ears like a piercing whistle. Tears were flowing down my cheeks even though I was coherent and able to speak. I said, "Why me?"

Lorraine stood by my side.

"Do you know what caused this to happen?" I stuttered.

She said, softly, "A number of things can: lack of nourishment, disease, sickness, improper medications."

My eyes flicked toward Lorraine's, then, instinctively, I said, "Several months ago I was treated for amoebic dysentery, and an Indian doctor gave me some strong medication that I had a bad reaction to. Could that have caused this?"

The doctor dipped her head with a twinge of anger in her eyes. "Yes, it very well could have."

All my medals of valor could not restrain the tears and anger flaring in my face. Seconds later my inner rebellion ceased like a flame extinguished by water.

The ride back to Long Beach was, in the words of one poet, "an endless tear." I felt betrayed by God one moment and filled with faith and courage the next.

We decided to wait until Mark was released from the hospital to tell him. This was possible because the specialist had advised me to carry the baby until the pregnancy had run its course so the child could be delivered through natural means.

I couldn't look at Mark when I relayed the terrible news. I felt like I had failed him. The son he had wanted for so long had been snatched from him. Mark rested my head on his shoulder and let me hide my eyes against his neck.

"It's okay," he said, weaving his hand through my hair. "It's okay. I love you. Everything's going to be all right." Tears began rinsing his cheeks as he repeated, "Everything's all right."

Two weeks later, at eight o'clock in the morning, I entered the hospital with labor pains. An attractive nurse wheeled me to the elevator and asked, "Do you want a boy or girl?"

"It really doesn't matter," I said, finishing the sentence to myself . . . because it's dead.

Mark entered the room like a walking figure from a wax museum. He was pleasant, but it was clearly a mask. Underneath the facade, tears were drenching his face. He, too, dreaded my impending pain. Knowing the difficulties that can arise in a birth of this nature, my physician had cancelled all her appointments that day so she could be nearby.

Twelve hours after being admitted—taunting hours of doubt and despair—labor finally commenced. During the delivery I regained consciousness only long enough to feel the doctor extracting pieces of the placenta. Fear flash-flooded through my nervous system, then, just as quickly, I fell asleep.

As the orderlies wheeled me from the recovery room some time later, Mark raced down the corridor to overtake the gurney.

Grabbing my hand, he asked, "How are you feeling?"

"Still a little drowsy."

"God answered prayer today; you're going to be all right."

With that reassuring thought, once again I drifted off to sleep.

At two o'clock in the morning, I awoke to excruciating back pains. The physician on duty diagnosed kidney failure. I was afraid this scene might be my final act because of the way the nurses and doctors were scurrying about.

Crying out to God, I said, "Forgive me for doubting You. Please, God, touch my body and make me well so I can help Mark raise the money he needs to build a school."

By seven o'clock the next morning, the doctor announced the kidney malfunction had corrected *itself.* But I knew it was *my Father in heaven* who had reached down His hand to help a desperate woman like me.

# 26
## *Courageous Huldah?*

From my hospital bed, I said, "Mark, go ahead and meet with the Assemblies officials in Springfield. We need their approval for the school and if you don't see them this time, it may be another four months before the officials meet."

"I'm not sure I should leave you," he countered.

"I'll be fine, go ahead."

Indecisively, Mark lowered his head in thought, not wanting to shrug his responsibilities to me yet realizing the importance of the meeting.

After kissing me, he left for the airport that afternoon and promised to return as soon as possible.

I wanted him to go. He had to go. I knew that. But loneliness gripped me like a noose. "God, why does he have to leave now when I need him the most?"

Six consecutive days, while Mark was away, a local minister—a friend of ours—entered my hospital room with encouraging sermonettes. He said, "Sister Buntain, God only allows these things to happen to people He can trust."

I thanked the reverend. Still, I couldn't help but wonder what conceivable purpose could be served by the death of an unborn child.

During those six days that Mark was away, self-pity moved in like a long lost friend. I almost detested the sight of white sheets, flowers, nurses, white caps, and that smell unique to a hospital. Everything reminded me of the innocent baby who had, presumably, been bludgeoned by a doctor's needle bearing improper medication.

Ed and Alice, who had been caring for Bonnie at their home in La Crescenta, California, entered my room like celestial cherubim at a time when tragedy and death surrounded me. They had come to rescue me from this lonely incarceration and take me home.

When Mark returned from his Springfield summit, his face flushed as I inquired about his meeting.

I asked, "Can we raise the money to build the school?"

He tilted his head to cloak his feelings. "They didn't say we couldn't build a school, but they want us to build a Bengali church first."

Although I understood and respected the Assemblies' priority on evangelism, I was naturally disappointed.

Attempting to change the subject, Mark asked, "How are you feeling?"

"I'm okay." I wouldn't let him desert my inquiry about the school. "How can we raise that kind of money?"

Resolve mounted in Mark's jaw. "I don't know, but just as God built our church, He'll help us build the Bengali church *and* a school."

I noted to myself, And you're going to kill yourself trying to raise that money, aren't you? You'd build the Taj Mahal if God told you to. I knew that raising the money we needed meant holding meetings almost every night. Nevertheless, Mark had faith that God would help him accomplish the task. Sometimes I wondered if he was simply a man of faith or a crazed preacher with unlimited determination.

While I recuperated at Ed and Alice's, Mark began traveling from church to church to share the desperate need for a school and a Bengali church.

One evening after a Sunday service, Ed and Alice were enjoying a time of fellowship with members of their church while Mark was away. Mark's mother, Bonnie, and I were enveloped by solitude. I closed the door to my bedroom and collapsed onto the bed in tears. I had tried to be strong, the epitome of a stalwart Christian. But the grief brought on by loneliness and self-pity was more than I could bear alone, and it spilled from my lips with squeals resembling those of an animal caught in a bear trap.

I cried Mark's name repeatedly until his mother stampeded into my room and wrapped me in her arms with surprising strength. Ed and Alice soon arrived and sat up for several hours listening to my rambling pains.

By the time Mark drove into the driveway three days later, I was "courageous Huldah" again, free of depression and ready to do whatever was necessary to build a school.

Once I had regained my strength, our calendar rivaled that of a corporate president. We embarked on a pilgrimage that would take us across the provinces and states of North America to share our vision for India.

In the middle of a congested highway one sunny afternoon, I said, "Mark, I'm a little concerned about you. How long can you keep this pace up? You're already exhausted. You're not going to do Calcutta much good if you're in a hospital."

With disarming honesty, he said, "Sure I'm tired. You are, too. This is just something we have to do. God wants that school and church built."

Bonnie interrupted from the back seat, "You know what?"

I played along. "What?"

"There's no such thing as God."

I asked politely, "Honey, why do you say that?"

"'Cause, if there was a God, He wouldn't have let my baby brother die. I prayed so long for a brother or sister."

"Listen to me real good, okay?"

She nodded and looked at me with wide eyes.

"We don't know why God allowed our baby to die. He could have stopped it from happening, but He didn't. And no one but God knows why. But that doesn't mean He's not alive in heaven."

"I guess not," the youngster said. "If I was God, I wouldn't let nobody die."

"Why don't we pray to God together right now?" I suggested.

Bonnie cupped her hands together, closed her eyes, and prayed in her high-pitched voice, "Dear Jesus, please give me another brother. Amen."

Mark and I looked at one another, then, simultaneously, we let out a therapeutic chuckle.

# 27
# *"Don't Give Up!"*

Mark wished he could have stayed longer in the States to raise more funding, but our furlough had come to a close. Bonnie, on the other hand, was anxious to return to Calcutta despite the intrigue of seeing ice cubes, escalators, hot dogs, and garden salads for the first time. She had grown weary of attending church services night after night where she was asked to speak Hindi for the amusement of others.

We loaded our luggage, including a donated organ, onto the Dutch ship with intentions of flying to meet the vessel in Singapore. But our connecting flight from Hawaii to Hong Kong was delayed. The airline company, at its expense, put us in a motel room for several hours and promised to send a vehicle to collect us when the plane was ready to depart.

We were sleeping ever so soundly when it dawned on us that the airline may have forgotten to pick us up. We rushed to the airport only to see our jetliner lifting off.

As a result, again, all at the airline's expense, we spent another day lounging around the pool in Hawaiian shirts and eating pineapple in this Polynesian paradise before continuing on to Calcutta. God does have a way of making up for some of the trials of travel.

When we tried to board our ship in Singapore, we sensed the captain's reluctance to welcome us aboard. He explained later that a group of missionaries—passengers from the States to Singapore—had offended the other travelers. They had prayed loudly, preached on deck, and condemned everyone for drinking alcohol. So, when the passengers learned we were missionaries as well, they had pleaded with the captain to prevent us from boarding the ship.

But it didn't take long for us to extinguish the fears of the other passengers. We conversed with them on deck, drank sodas, and were cordial.

The captain came to Mark soon after we were settled in our quarters. He told Mark about a young man going to India to join an ashram to become a sadu—a Hindu priest. "He's confused. Could you talk with him?" the captain asked. "We can't seem to get through to him. Maybe you can."

Throughout the voyage Mark saw as much of the moon as he did the sun, for he and Roger—this young man—stayed awake every night discussing the Bible.

By the time we docked in Calcutta, Roger had accepted Christ. The Hindu priests were there waiting for him when we deboarded, but Roger sent them away. Some months later the young man returned to his homeland, anxious to share what he had traveled halfway around the world to discover—that Jesus Christ died for his sins.

The population of Calcutta seemed to have multiplied. Thousands wandered about with no apparent destination. I didn't think it was possible, but as I walked through the bustees there appeared to be twice as many sick children and under-nourished beggars.

Glancing at my husband, I noticed that twice as many lines furrowed Mark's face. His cheeks had sagged. His eyes were puffy like a boxer who had just lost a fifteen round decision. According to the doctors, my husband was suffering from mental and physical exhaustion. They confined him to bed. But it was no use; invariably, a telephone or pen materialized in his hand and he continued to work even from bed. Consequently, he was sent to Childer's Lodge in the Himalayan Mountains—an inn run by Christian friends, Leon and Almeda Elliott.

"What's wrong with me?" he had asked prior to his departure.

"Nothing," I had responded, "you're just overworked." I hoped and prayed that was *all* it was.

The Longs were still serving as interim pastors at our church so at least Mark could rest knowing the work was in capable hands. Because Bonnie had to go to school, I could not accompany Mark to the lodge. My loyalty was divided, torn between obligations to Mark, Bonnie, and the church, wondering every hour if my beleaguered husband needed me.

Then a call from the Elliotts gave me the answer I was searching for. Mark had not improved, so he had been admitted into a hospital.

Immediately, I made plans to leave the next morning by train for Mussoorie where Mark was staying. I had just kissed Bonnie good night when suddenly a shattering of glass bolted me from her bedside into the hallway. The Noritake chinaware that Mark had brought from the Orient years earlier had fallen from its shelves and lay before me like a puzzle of a thousand pieces.

"Why?" I cried.

Bonnie entered only to see me in tears. I hugged her to my waist and stood in place until the misery evaporated. The mess before me mirrored what I feared was happening to our lives. Recognizing that the enemy was the source of this heartless object lesson helped to ease my despondency and panic. Then an image of my mother's pear jars grazed my thoughts, and my tears ceased. I began picking up the shattered fragments, believing God was going to do the same for our lives.

At dawn, in May, 1961, my eight-year-old and I boarded the train and were ushered to our four-berth compartment. As I sat there, ready to embark on a two-day journey, I stared endlessly. Since this was my first trip on the "rail" without Mark, I was too frightened to talk to anyone. At least Bonnie was with me, I thought, but she soon drifted off to sleep. I made a pillow of my lap for her head.

Within miles, the smell of perspiration was stretching my level of endurance. A puddle of sweat from my arms and legs formed on the metal floor. In the center of the open room of compartments a block of ice was placed to combat the heat. We were the only Caucasians aboard, which had never before worried me, but the scanning eyes of several men reminded me of stories I had heard about thieves robbing women of their jewelry while they slept. Secretly, I ran through a sequence of prayers then, well before nightfall, Bonnie and I climbed into our bunk to get some rest.

When we arrived at the hospital, Mark was asleep. Dr. Wertz, a Baptist worker, motioned for me to join him outside.

"Thank you for coming so quickly, Mrs. Buntain. I'm afraid your husband is suffering from severe fatigue, and unless he learns to rest, he's not going to live long. We've taken away his Bible and preaching tapes. He has the body of a seventy-year-old. He's not sleeping without sedatives, and we can't get him to eat. Please, take him back to Canada or the United States," the doctor urged morosely.

"I can't. He has raised money to build a school and church. I know him; he won't go back until they're completed."

"Understand what I'm saying. Either he slows down or he isn't going to be around to build anything."

I thanked the doctor then slouched in a chair in the hallway. My disbelieving ears could hear the faint hum of moaning patients. My eyes couldn't focus for a moment. The invincible man with the mountains of faith and energy was bedridden, fighting to recover. I wondered if I would soon be burying him in the graveyard below the hospital where other missionaries had been laid to rest.

I closed my eyes and quietly spoke: "God, I've prayed for Mark many times before. Every time You've answered my prayers. I'm coming to You again. I don't know what to do. If You want us to build that school and hospital, please restore his health. Reach down and help him."

Mark, in the meantime, appeared to be weakening. He had lost weight, and his face was as pale as an Orient pearl. He seldom spoke, but when he did his words were miscalculated.

"God has forsaken me. Take Bonnie and go back to Vancouver. Leave me to die."

"Don't talk like that," I said sternly.

"It's the truth," he rasped.

"Listen, Mark, you have to get well so we can build that school. Do what the doctor tells you. Take as much time as you need to get better. Don't let the enemy keep you from doing God's work. Don't give up!"

For days, as I made the journey back and forth to Mark's side through the bush overgrowth on the hill between Childer's Lodge and the mission hospital, I found myself praying and repeating Deuteronomy 33:27: "The eternal God is your refuge, and underneath are the everlasting arms."

Then almost as if someone was walking beside me one evening, I heard a voice say, "Finish the verse."

I turned, but no one was there.

I kept walking, wondering whether it was just my imagination, or if I had really heard Someone say, "Finish the verse."

I realized that I had quoted only part of the verse, for it finished with a promise: "And He will thrust out the enemy from before you." Then I knew God had spoken to my heart and given me the assurance that Mark would recover.

At dusk one evening, that verse seemed far too appropriate for the danger I found myself in. A large cat with huge green eyes that glowed in the dark sat in my path as I strode to Childer's Lodge. Its feet were bent as if ready to pounce at me. I stood still, stared, and invited the Bible verse to race through my mind again. Finally the animal retreated.

The subsequent days crept by slowly. Then, almost like the biblical Lazarus being raised from the dead, Mark began to steadily improve.

When the doctors discharged him from the hospital, he was still weak but beginning to stand tall, knowing God had helped him to overcome an attack of the enemy.

# 28
## Peaks and Valleys

Some weeks later, after Mark had fully recovered, we returned to Calcutta with a renewed determination to build a school. But in order to build the school, it was paramount that the Muslim land owner sell us a back portion of his lot on Royd Street. He wasn't eager to release it, though, and we feared another drawn-out negotiation awaited us.

Mark was summoned to the owner's bedside one afternoon, only to discover the man was deathly ill. Mark took the man's hand and prayed. Then, just minutes after Mark left, the man died. Superstitious as they were, the sons agreed to sell the property to Mark because he was the last one to speak to their father.

Getting them to sell the real estate was the first hurdle; the second was raising the funds to buy it. Nevertheless, we believed God would provide.

Because of our financial need, Mark had called a deacons' prayer meeting one evening. He was plodding wearily up to our flat at eleven o'clock at night when I greeted him at the top of the stairs, declaring, "You can end your prayers. The money is on its way!" Mark peered at me starkly, his expression dangling between a smile and tears.

I said, "I have a cable in my hand from Alice saying that the funds are going to be sent to buy the property."

Mark read the cable, then shouted, "Hallelujah!"

A layman in Ed's church had asked Alice if something in particular was troubling her brother. Alice told the man about our financial crisis, and within days he had wired what was needed to purchase the land.

For Mark and I it was as if God, through this miracle, repeated His vow to never forsake us. In response, all we could do was wrap our arms around one another and sigh a prayer of thanksgiving and relief into the other's ear.

Philosophers have said that life is an endless horizon of peaks and valleys. I was ready to espouse that philosophy myself—hoping we were about to enjoy some peaks—when construction finally started on the school.

My administrative responsibilities began to steadily increase with the growth of the church and the establishment of a school. I usually didn't abdicate my household chores to someone else, but an unusual arrangement fell into our laps. Our good friends and neighbors, the Baileys, had been transferred to England. They had offered to give their apartment to the church if we agreed to hire their cooks. Acceptable living quarters like their apartment were almost impossible to find in the city, so we had to take advantage of this opportunity. I needed assistance with my hectic schedule, and we wanted to help this Indian couple by giving them employment.

Their son, Krishna, who was three days older than Bonnie, soon became like a brother to our daughter. They played by the hour together. He ate at our table and slept in one of our beds. I taught him to tie his shoelaces, and I tucked him in each night. Mark even bought him gifts on his birthday, which was celebrated each year along with Bonnie's.

God smiled on us again when evangelist Kathryn Kuhlman came to Calcutta. Miss Kuhlman couldn't bear to see us suffering without an air conditioner, so she had our entire flat—the same one the Maroccos had lived in—re-wired and an air conditioner installed. She even sent us on a vacation to South India to enjoy an animal reserve filled with black tigers, elephants, and lions.

Surely God was with us. I knew He was always by our sides, but at times I had permitted devastating circumstances to plant seeds of skepticism.

At this stage in our lives, however, Mark and I were overwhelmed with optimism. The construction of the school had progressed on schedule, and a charitable organization had granted us two hundred student sponsorships—many that previously had been earmarked for a school that was now closed.

God had also provided a precious Indian-born female principal with vast experience. Shortly after Mrs. Shaw began attending an Assemblies of God church, Mark hired her to oversee our education program. She was a gifted woman who was strong in the Lord and possessed unlimited faith. Her six children were all very intelligent as well. Some years later, her son, Ron Shaw, and his wife, Felicia, returned from studying at Bethany Bible College to become key leaders in the mission. Ron served as our senior associate of the English speaking church. Felicia, a registered nurse, was instrumental in establishing our first small hospital.

More than five hundred invitations were sent out for the dedication of the school facility. Mark and I would long remember that day in January, 1964—a day to recognize what God had accomplished. But as the dedication approached, political riots broke out in the city that were similar to the campus riots of the 1960s in the United States. Word of the fighting swept to the West, and one by one, our out-of-town guests canceled their plans to be with us. Naturally we were disappointed, yet who could blame them for not wanting to brave the violence engulfing the city?

The decorations and tables of food were enjoyed by only a small gathering of people that day. But among the heavenly hosts, I decided, there must have been an exuberant, largely attended celebration.

Shortly after the dedication, Mark was struck with pneumonia and had to be hospitalized. Bonnie had a near-fatal bout with high fever that turned into tropical measles. I feared the enemy was on the warpath again, but our family was not his only target. Later in 1964, the city was besieged with disastrous floods, leaving thousands homeless and hungry. The church fed scores of refugees while the waters stagnated above clogged drains for weeks.

Largely because of the flood, we expanded our feeding program but realized that we had merely scratched the surface. Somehow, we had to do more to nourish the hungry and treat the diseased. The hospitals were overcrowded and understaffed, and several children had fainted in the classroom from malnutrition. We knew we had to do more.

With that goal in mind, Mark and Bonnie and I returned to the States in 1966 to begin raising support for a hospital, our feeding program, and the school.

Bonnie regretted having to leave behind her animals— several pets that inhabited our veranda: a spider monkey, a squirrel that had once crawled into my closet and chewed a hole in one of my dresses, an array of fish, a parakeet, two dogs, and the two guinea pigs she had painted green with water coloring.

She was also sorry to leave Mrs. Blinkworth who had come to live with us as Bonnie's babysitter. She was an English woman we had taken in while she was undergoing treatment for some severe dental problems. The elderly woman moved in for a temporary recuperation period and stayed for several years. Mrs. Blinkworth was a blessing to us, especially since Mark and I often had to work late or attend evening church services. With a war raging on the Chinese border, we took comfort in knowing Bonnie was in good hands when the air-raid sirens sounded, the city experienced blackouts, and the streets were in chaos.

Bonnie's reluctance to leave also came from her dislike of constantly traveling and being on display like a carnival attraction in the churches we visited. In the past we had marched her up on the platform in her Indian costume and had her greet the congregations in Hindi and in her British-accented English. I'm sure she felt like a ventriloquist's dummy at times. But now that she was thirteen, we promised not to do that. Instead, she would attend school in Vancouver and live with Uncle Lionel and Mother while we traveled weeks at a time without her.

Uncle Lionel had fixed the basement in his house as a game room for Bonnie. She thoroughly enjoyed his company, but she cried whenever we left for an extended time. Sometimes I wondered if our desire to build a hospital was worth the tumultuous schedule and the weeks of separation from our daughter.

Mark agonized over unanswered questions when, at first, his plan for a large hospital in downtown Calcutta was rejected. He longed to build a high-rise medical center that would proclaim God's concern for the whole man. For weeks he had shared stories of children fainting in classrooms, patients sharing beds in Indian hospitals, and reports of crows and rats invading hospital rooms. Congregations were moved by the truthful scenes he painted with his words. But now the hope of his heart—a hospital—seemed very much in doubt.

Those were solemn weeks as we traveled the highways of North America. Mark often chose to draw within himself rather than to expose his disappointment and discouragement.

As we drove along, new ideas began to surface. We talked about the situation we had left behind in Calcutta where our home had become a makeshift treatment center and an orphanage, too. Some evenings we had returned from church to find our bed occupied by one of the sickly "patrons" who had assumed residence. We both knew *something* had to be done. We could start a clinic in the rear of the church and establish mobile units that could go into the surrounding villages. If we couldn't build a hospital, at least we could spend this furlough raising funds for the next best thing.

# 29
## *Mother of Many*

On a monsoon-like night Mark and Bonnie made their way to Calcutta's airport to meet Suzie Dillingham's plane. Lightning flashed dangerously across the sky, and rain pelted the car's windshield with a vengeance.

Our friendship with the Dillinghams had grown over the years. Their daughter Suzie was Bonnie's age, and the two girls had a lot in common. Because the missionary couple was still on furlough in the States, Suzie had returned to India ahead of her parents so she could begin school on time. After spending a few days with us, she would catch a flight to Bangalore.

Mark and Bonnie were anxiously watching the tarmac when the pilot missed the runway and the aircraft burst into flames. The 707 jetliner landed in a rice field. Passengers fled the wreckage in darkness as the fire crew rushed to the crash site with its sirens blaring.

Since Mark and the girls had not returned, I assumed the nasty weather had delayed Suzie's flight. But a telephone call from Mark conveyed the agonizing details.

"It was an awful sight! A hundred feet from the runway the plane crashed. But they tell me everyone escaped."

A portrait of Suzie's frightful fate flashed before me. "My God!" I exclaimed, too shocked to even cry. "Where is she?"

"We're at one of the hospitals now. We can't find her anywhere. I'll call you when we do."

Several hours passed. Then Bonnie burst through the door ranting with tears flowing down her cheeks. I bounced to my feet and held her in my arms.

I was afraid to ask *the* question.

Mark walked into the room, his raincoat draped over his arm. He had been crying, too.

Bonnie blurted, "The plane exploded. Suzie's dead."

I looked at Mark hoping it wasn't so.

He said, "They found her body trapped in the rear of the plane. Six of the sixty-three passengers were killed."

The next few evenings I had trouble sleeping. All I could think about was Suzie. The blond child was so full of life. Her blue eyes and dimples brought joy wherever she went. I couldn't believe she would never again brighten our home or play with our daughter.

I spent my waking hours mourning and reminiscing about the times we had nearly lost Bonnie. When she was quite young, she was struck with a severe case of the measles, and her temperature rose to 105 degrees. We put ice packs on her body and prayed by the hour. Soon the fever broke, and her life was spared. At age twelve she needed an emergency appendectomy while Mark was away visiting needy villagers. I thought of the frightful episode when she climbed the staircase to the terrace in Jamshedpur and the time in Ceylon when she stuck her finger in a fan. When she contracted a severe case of hepatitis, I feared for her life before God healed her.

For the Dillinghams none of that mattered. No hero had come to the rescue of their daughter. I grieved for Suzie's parents, knowing they had lost their most precious possession. They were unable to attend the funeral for fear they would jeopardize their visas, so I did my best to handle the arrangements as if Suzie were my own daughter.

Even after the funeral, Suzie Dillingham kept surfacing in my thoughts: her parents, their sorrow, the irreplaceable years of laughter and warm embraces. I continued to think of Bonnie—our gift-child—and the many nights I hadn't been there to tuck her in. I had never taught her how to sew or cook, and someone else had helped her with her homework. Now she was a teenager, and the days of playing on the floor and telling bedtime stories were a fading dream. Had I been so concerned with the souls of Calcutta that I had neglected my own flesh and blood?

As she was growing up, I made certain Bonnie knew we loved her. Little things like using the good china for a mother and daughter dinner or taking her shopping were special times for both of us. Still, Bonnie's home life obviously differed from that of her peers back in Canada and the United States. We knew some missionary children who felt neglected and had developed resentment toward their parents. Mark and I went to great lengths to express our love and to point out that she was, in fact, privileged to be a missionary's daughter—able to see the world and experience other cultures while accomplishing something substantial for God.

While Bonnie had no brothers or sisters of her own, she was never without a playmate. In fact, she often had to share a room with the less fortunate children her father carried into our flat. Our "inn" was full, but somehow we always found a place on the floor for one more person Mark had rescued from the shadows of secluded alleys. Bonnie, fortunately, didn't seem to mind sharing her parents or her home. Somehow she had developed her own heart of compassion.

Our apartment frequently resembled an American slumber party. We strung cots from wall to wall to accomodate everybody—only our guests weren't wearing the plush pajamas customary in the West. Their clothes were often crusted and torn. When their calloused, flat feet entered our home for the first time, their hair was often matted and infested with lice and their faces were smudged with dirt and grease. Many required treatment for wounds and sickness.

Under the stairs of our flat lived a little boy and his father. He often peeked in our car window as our vehicle braked in front of our building. Mark sometimes reached out and tousled the boy's hair, which made the lad smile. One day I saw the boy alone, shivering, cradling himself in their dark cubicle. Coming closer, I noticed a huge abscess on the side of his neck. We rushed him to a hospital for treatment, but the physician offered little hope for survival. Mark and I prayed anyway, and the boy gradually regained his health.

With his father's permission, we enrolled the boy in a boarding school. The boy's father died shortly thereafter and, from that day on, we did what we could to care for him.

Sometime later, the boy's mother, who had been separated from his father for many years, also died. She had a reputation in the community as a loan shark who loaned money at exorbitant interest rates.

After her death we heard that the lad, who was now a sixteen-year-old, was trying to collect her debts by threatening the poor borrowers with arrest. When I heard of his insensitivity and ingratitude, I naturally scolded him, pointing out all we had done for him without expecting payment.

He said, "Who do you think you are telling me what I can and can't do? You're not my mother!"

Like an enraged parent I began walloping him with a book I was holding in my hand.

His head dropped, then he fell to his knees crying. "You really love me, don't you?" he said, lifting his head from his humble position.

"Of course, I love you. That's why we've cared for you all these years. I want you to be educated and make something of your life."

"No, tonight is the first time you spanked me like your own child . . . the first night I knew you really loved me."

Under the street lamp that evening I embraced him as a son, realizing I truly was the mother of many.

# 30
# *A Long Distance Marriage*

Streamers were strung from one corner of our apartment to the other, and balloons were hung from the walls. Some teenagers had walked a long distance just to attend the celebration. An invitation to a birthday party where cake and ice cream were to be served was like being invited to the Inaugural Ball. I wanted to make Bonnie's sixteenth birthday a day she would always remember.

Mark was preaching in the villages and had not returned, so we cut the cake without him. An hour passed; then another. No sign of Mark. Some children were already leaving.

About 10:30 p.m., after all the decorations had been torn down and all the children had left, Mark slipped into our apartment like a cat burglar afraid of getting caught red-handed.

"Where have you been?" I frowned.

"In the villages. Why?"

"You don't remember what we had planned tonight?" He thought for a moment. "Oh no! Bonnie's birthday."

Venting my disgust, I said, "How could you forget? I told you just yesterday."

"Is she already in bed?" Mark asked, his eyes drooping with shame.

"Yes."

Mark tip-toed to her room, and from the door I eavesdropped as he apologized to his yawning daughter.

Moments later, once he had climbed into bed, I said, "I know you have a lot on your mind, but Bonnie deserves more of our attention."

"I know she does. She's getting older, and we don't have many years left before she goes away to college."

My head lifted from my pillow. "Well, why can't she stay here in Calcutta? She can go to college here."

Mark said, "We'll talk about it later." He rolled over to sleep, leaving me to discuss Bonnie's future without him.

Early in our marriage, out of necessity, I learned to function without my husband by my side. His ministry had taken him all over the world, often without me, so it was either learn to survive alone or throw in the towel. I wholeheartedly believed if he was to succeed in the ministry and pursue God's plan, I needed to give him freedom, support, and encouragement. It wasn't always easy for me to accept that premise, yet I knew this was *our* ministry together, even if we frequently ate and slept on opposite corners of the globe.

My deep love for Mark made the periods of separation more difficult. And sometimes I didn't cope well with our partitioned lives. One evening, in particular, yielded sheer misery. It should have been one of the most memorable evenings of my life. Instead, I dreaded the dawning of that day. It was our twenty-fifth wedding anniversary—a milestone— but Mark and I were separated by an ocean of water. He had been asked to speak at a large convention in Denver, so I consented to let him go.

That night gloom enveloped me. Not even Bonnie's presence or the assurance Mark loved me could brighten the dreary atmosphere of desolation. Tears of depression flowed.

The scars of sustained sacrifice raised their ugly head, and I was consumed by despair. But in my lonely hour, God reminded me that He was near, that He loved me, and that He understood my feelings. Only then was the gloom dispelled.

When Mark returned, he surprised me with a beautiful ring and apologized remorsefully for his absence. I responded as if I understood. And I did understand. But sometimes understanding and acceptance are inadequate to soothe the inner turmoil of being separated from the one you love. Sometimes only God can give us peace.

# 31
## Bonnie

A screenwriter could not have penned a more touching, poignant scene than Mark bidding farewell to his little girl. Just before Bonnie and I boarded the plane to enroll her in Evangel College in Springfield, Missouri, Mark held her for a long while, almost refusing to let her go but knowing that he must. Her long blond hair was pinned against the nape of her neck, beneath his affectionate hand. Their faces looked like they had been splashed with tears as they parted.

"I love you," he called as she walked toward the gate. "I love you, I'll miss you."

As we climbed the ladder to our aircraft, I could almost hear him calling and calling, as if he was trying to make up for lost time. At Mark's insistence Bonnie had enrolled in an American college. Now that his little girl was actually leaving, however, regret suddenly registered on his face.

As we deboarded in Springfield, I felt the sun's rays warm my skin and the pure oxygen dart through my lungs. What an exhilarating feeling!

We were invited to the home of Jim and Velma Long, missionaries to India, where Bonnie and their son Jim Jr. were meeting on quite different terms this time around. What a difference a decade had made. Jim Jr. didn't have much to do with Bonnie when they were in Calcutta together as children. He was more interested in playing with plastic models, and he balked at his mother's orders to escort Bonnie and his sister to school. Now, however, I could see a thread of infatuation weaving its way through their conversation.

Jim, a handsome young man, was also attending Evangel College.

"What courses are you taking?" he asked, his blond bangs shielding his forehead.

Bonnie listed her classes and then confessed her concern over chemistry.

"I'm a student teacher in chemistry. I would be happy to help you!" Jim exclaimed.

He then realized he had exhibited an overabundance of enthusiasm and quickly retracted his voice like a musical decrescendo.

As I watched the two youngsters' eyes perk, it suddenly occurred to me just how mature my girl had become. I wished I could keep her at seventeen—an age where she had the vitality of youth and the blossoming mind of an adult. She had become my friend, my companion. And the thought of her wearing an engagement ring from some young man was almost inconceivable.

Because she never had much of a social life in Calcutta, I had advised Bonnie to get well-acquainted with a boy before accepting a date. Furthermore, I suggested she go out with various boys so she could develop a better idea of what she was looking for in a spouse.

The afternoon following our visit with the Longs, Bonnie and I filed into the enrollment line at the college. I didn't realize that the institution's policy required students to make a sizable down payment on their tuition. We didn't have the money the college was requesting, and I could see terror and embarrassment rising in Bonnie's eyes.

Understanding our predicament, the dean suggested I call a pastor in Denver who had provided scholarships to needy students. Without one persuasive word from me, this pastor awarded Bonnie a scholarship over the phone.

When it finally came time for me to return to Calcutta, Bonnie and I cried into each other's arms. I knew our relationship would never be the same. She would undergo changes and become more independent. The little pony-tailed Caucasian who once played among a quiver of brown children was just a memory. Bonnie Buntain was almost a grown woman, with dreams and aspirations of her own; she would never need me like she once had.

At the airport terminal that day, saying goodby was as traumatic as losing someone I loved.

As we embraced one final time, Bonnie said, "I'll miss you, Mom. I'll write you."

My face veiled in tears, I scampered away that comfortable fall day wondering when I would see her again and how much she would change in the meantime.

Some days I walked into what was once Bonnie's bedroom in Calcutta, and my sentimental emotions washed over me. When Mark was away and the house was unusually quiet, my heart yearned for my daughter to be closer. I worried about her almost nightly, wondering to myself if we had done the right thing by sending her so far away to a country so unfamiliar.

As the blistering days and months wore on, letters from Bonnie were frequent. Her correspondence indicated that she was having a difficult time adjusting. Reading between the lines, I also knew she was falling in love with Jim.

Jim and Bonnie had become closer when he began assisting her with her homework; in essence, he was her link to the English language, a subject she was struggling with. Even under Jim's watchful eye, Bonnie learned some lessons painfully. Unaware of the dangers of icy pavement, Bonnie slipped and broke her leg. Because she was unaccustomed to running hot water, she also burned herself in the shower. I began to realize just how unprepared my daughter was for life in America. After all, she had never used an automatic washer and dryer, purchased cosmetics, or taken English or American history classes.

Because of the expense, our telephone conversations with Bonnie were limited. When I did call her hall phone, sometimes at two o'clock in the morning Central Standard Time, I woke up the girls in her dormitory. And because of the static on the international lines, Bonnie would *keep* them awake by having to holler into the receiver.

During one such conversation her voice squeaked with fear as she admitted to me she didn't think she could survive the cultural and educational challenges. We prayed over the phone that night, "God, take Bonnie's hand right now and calm all her fears. Help her to feel comfortable and confident. Let her know You're with her."

Thereafter, Bonnie's outlook on college life changed. Not only was she learning to trust the Lord more, but she was growing more dependent on Jim. Wisely, he implored her to "be herself," and by her second semester it was apparent his message was finally beginning to sink in.

At the outset of Bonnie's second year, Mark and I returned to Springfield on furlough. Students were rushing to and from classes as we set foot on campus.

A young lady with long, stringy hair walked past us; at first glance, we didn't recognize her as our own daughter.

"Bonnie?" I called.

She turned, smiled, and dashed toward us with her arms spread wide.

After Mark and I gave Bonnie a warm embrace, I stepped back to take a look at my transformed daughter. It was difficult for me to assess the changes in her, but I knew they were there.

Unthinkable as it was, Bonnie seemed to distance herself from us in the coming weeks—even though she was genuinely elated that we were back in the United States. She was afraid of getting too close because she knew she would be losing us again once our short furlough ended. The thought of not seeing us again for three or four years made the present unbearable.

That entire stay, Mark and I zigzagged across North America raising funds and sharing the needs of India in churches of all sizes. When it was time to return to Calcutta, we had only spent several weeks with Bonnie, largely because she was preoccupied but partly because she could not risk resurrecting the emotional ties and dependency she had fought so hard to overcome.

Our six months in the United States and Canada—separated from Bonnie only by our obligations to the ministry—were soul-wrenching.

Mark's proposal for a large hospital was again rejected. While he was fighting the side-effects of that decision—discouragement and disbelief—I found myself alone recovering from a hysterectomy in an unfamiliar hospital in Vancouver, Canada. Mark was at a convention in Toronto, Bonnie was still in school, and Mother and Uncle Lionel were kept away by an imposing snowstorm. At first my spirits were invincible. But gradually visions of the lonely hours after the death of my baby settled before my eyes like fresh snow transforming to gray slush.

Again I questioned if the Buntains were paying too great a price for Calcutta, sacrificing for the sake of sacrificing, when luxury and comfort in our homeland were one decision away. I reflected on the speech I had made at the women's luncheon held in conjunction with the General Council meeting of the Assemblies of God in Oklahoma City. More than one thousand women heard me say:

"Sure we've sacrificed what other couples have, but we haven't sacrificed happiness. I wasn't called to the mission field, but I was called to be Mark Buntain's wife. I was reluctant at first to go overseas to Calcutta, but I did so out of obedience to my husband's calling. There have been struggles, and I've had to carry my share of the load. Mark has had the faith, but I have had the ulcers," I said laughingly. "But, in closing, I want to encourage you to throw yourselves into the ministry God has called you and your husband to."

After the speech, the women stood to their feet with applause. But now, while recuperating alone in a hospital room, the enemy sought to diminish God's accomplishments in Calcutta. I laid there, momentarily doubting my very own words to those women in Oklahoma City. The enemy wanted me to give in and deny the blessing of doing God's work among the hurting of India. The enemy whispered the sacrifices and hardships I had made in one ear, but my heavenly Father shouted His satisfaction in the other. Before long it was just God and me in that room; I had resisted the enemy, and he had fled from me.

Something profitable came of that furlough, however, for our admiration of Jim and his treatment of Bonnie swelled. She had become more self-assured, and we knew Jim's influence was largely responsible. We weren't surprised to discover their boyfriend-girlfriend relationship was blossoming into something more.

After her second year at Evangel College, Bonnie transferred to a school of nursing in Springfield. That led us to hope she would return to help us establish our hospital once her nurses' training was completed. But those dreams dismantled one evening when she phoned our flat in Calcutta.

"Mom, I have some wonderful news. Jim has asked me to marry him."

I held the phone away from my mouth, attempting to regain my scattering composure.

"Mom, did you hear me?" she asked in a hollow tone.

"Yes, honey."

"Aren't you excited?"

"Of course, but do you think you're ready? You haven't dated other boys enough to be sure he's the one."

"I know he's the one. We love each other. He's going to become a doctor."

"Have you discussed a wedding date?"

"Maybe in June in Vancouver, but I thought you'd be happy for me."

"I am. I just wish you'd give it more time."

"I know it's God's will, I love him, and nothing else matters."

As Mark ecstatically snatched the phone from my hand, memories of my conversations with my father glistened in my mind. I remembered how Dad had persuaded me to wait until my twentieth birthday to get married. Then I thought of Jim and how much we liked him and his family and how we couldn't have asked for a finer son-in-law. It was just difficult knowing Bonnie would belong to someone else. At least, I consoled myself, she won't be getting married for nine months.

Since I had such strong feelings, it caught me by surprise to learn several months later from one of our relatives that the wedding had been moved up to January. Thinking I was not consulted, I wore the crumpled chin of a jilted mother. I called Bonnie only to discover Mark had approved the arrangement while he was in the States, and neither his correspondence nor Bonnie's had made it into my hands.

The closer it came to their wedding day, January 18, 1975, the more comfortable and excited I became. The ceremony was beautiful, and they made an exceptional couple.

After we returned to Calcutta, the people of our church expressed a desire to host a reception in their honor. Six months after the wedding, Bonnie and Jim visited us in Calcutta. By the garlands of flowers, food, and decorations, our congregation obviously approved of Jim as well. Some members thought the marriage had been arranged, as is the custom in parts of India, since the eldest son was marrying an only daughter.

In a sense Mark and I also believed the marriage had been arranged—by a loving God who heard the prayers and knew the hearts of concerned parents.

# 32

# *"Nobody Wants Me"*

I had a phone in each hand when an Anglo-Indian woman knocked on my office door. "Come in," I said, lowering the phones against my breast. The woman was embarrassed that she had interrupted my conversations. On one phone I was trying to raise money for next week's feeding program, and on the other line I was speaking to our high school principal. I motioned for the woman and her tiny daughter to occupy the two seats in front of my desk while I finished.

As I hung up the phone, the woman said, "My name is Mrs. Chandler."

"Hello, my name is Mrs. Buntain." Then I said to the little girl, "What's yours?"

The woman looked down at her daughter and said in English, "This is my daughter, Larissa."

Leaning over my desk, I said, "Hi, Larissa. How are you?"

Her beautiful brown eyes, partially shielded by her curly jet-black hair, were vibrant but somewhat timid. I brushed the hair from her eyes and smiled warmly to disarm her trepidation.

"You're a lovely girl." Then I asked her mother, "What can I do for you?"

"My daughter needs to go to school. My husband is dead. And I have no money." I could tell by the woman's face she was not well. I later learned she had a heart condition.

I had heard sad accounts like this almost every day that week. Some were lies, but many stories left me limp and despairing. I felt inadequate to be the one determining which children would have an opportunity for a better life. In the first few years I hated myself for having to turn children and their parents away with the explanation that we had no more room. Now, because of overcrowding, I had resolved that I could only accept the most needy.

I looked at the girl, asking myself if we could squeeze one more child into the feeding lines, if we could locate a desk for her to sit at, if we could find her new clothing to supplant the rags slung over her bony shoulders.

"I ask nothing for myself. Please help Larissa," the woman begged, prompting her to sob then cough.

I had seen so much poverty in my years in Calcutta. I wondered if I had grown so accustomed to the suffering that I could turn this lovely child away. It's better that we have children wall to wall than to let this child go without an education, I told myself.

"Yes," I finally blurted, running my hand along the side of the child's face. "She can enter our school."

The sincere mother leaned down and kissed her daughter's hidden forehead and said, "Larissa, you're safe now."

The young girl, for the first time since she entered my office, dared to smile.

Months later little Larissa barged into my office with startling news. We had become close friends since she first enrolled in our school. She occasionally came to my office to report how well she was doing in class, but it was obvious by her tears this was not a social call.

"My Mommy and Daddy are both dead, and now nobody wants me," she wailed. As she spoke, the little suitcase that contained her worldly possessions slipped from her hand and dropped to the floor.

"Come here," I said, reaching out my arms to the little girl. "We want you. I'll be your Mommy, and Pastor will be your Daddy."

Larissa immediately cuddled up to me like a purring kitten.

At home that evening, I said, "Mark, since Larissa's mother is gone, I think she should live with us." He nodded his approval, knelt down, and said to Larissa, "I believe you're the prettiest little girl in the world."

The five-year-old acknowledged his acceptance into the family by bouncing onto his lap with a wide grin.

As the weeks passed, we discovered, to our dismay, that the little girl had inherited some filthy language and bad habits while her mother was ill. My chiding did little to transform her vocabulary, so I resorted to using soap to wash out her mouth whenever an inappropriate superlative echoed from her lips.

"Stick out your tongue," I ordered.

Larissa obeyed.

After washing her tongue, I said, "Now ask Jesus to wash your heart."

She knelt and prayed. Then we hugged each other as if nothing had ever happened. With Bonnie away, Larissa became a much needed ally—someone I could pour my love into when Mark was out on one of his many ministry trips to isolated villages.

Losing Larissa was a thought I couldn't accept. She had lived with us for nearly four years, and now an American family had contacted us about the possibility of adopting her. As shades of fear and loneliness manifested themselves, my reluctance to let her go only increased.

Since our boys' home had been started, there weren't as many running, shouting, and fighting children around our apartment. I no longer felt like the mother of hundreds. I hadn't realized that their rambunctious behavior and pestering questions were a remedy for my lonely, tired evenings away from my family. I missed tying their shoelaces and washing their hair.

I was so thankful that Larissa was living with us. The thought of her adoption brought back memories of Bonnie's departure. Pondering the emptiness, the loneliness, and the unbearable serenity made my heart ache. Deep inside I hoped the adoption proceedings would fade away like a coastal fog at midday in Vancouver.

Six months passed before Larissa and I boarded an airplane for St. Louis, where she would rendezvous with her new family. The Mannings were marvelous, kind people. Larissa could not have had a better home. I knew this was God's will, but that didn't alleviate the pain I felt when Larissa and her new family drove away from the airport that day. I can still remember the look on her face as she waved goodbye from the rear window.

The subsequent weeks were, as expected, unmerciful. Mark was away, and the silence in our apartment was deafening. Sometimes I sat next to our window just to hear the whirlpool of traffic in the streets below. Often I worked into the early morning hours, burying my lonesome feelings within the financial reports, memos, and backlogged correspondence strung across our bed. In those quiet hours alone in our apartment, I couldn't see the crowded auditoriums stateside or hear Mark's stirring messages to village congregations. I just had to imagine them with satisfaction from afar and pray God would help me persevere one day at a time without Bonnie or Larissa or the man I loved.

Each time Mark walked through our doors from an extended ministry tour, I gave him a monarch's reception. One such homecoming I asked, "Mark, what would you think about adopting Maureen before we leave on furlough?" Maureen was an eight-year-old who lived in a boarding school and had spent many of her weekends playing with

Larissa in our home. She had a smile that could don the covers of teenage magazines. Her mother, who was a widow and had a large family, had requested that we enroll her tiny daughter in a boarding school where she could receive adequate care.

Mark had always been fond of the little girl, so he approved of my suggestion without hesitation. Within weeks, Maureen Buntain became an official member of our family. When I tucked our new daughter into her very own bed on that first night, she smiled at me as if I were a fairy godmother there to bestow riches beyond her imagination. I grinned at her, too, thanking God for such a special gift. I couldn't wait to take her with us on furlough to introduce her to the rest of her new family.

# 33
## *You Pray—
## I'll Worry*

Every night as Mark and I prayed for a hospital, his words were primed with urgency and tears often cascaded into his heavy hands. When he fasted for days, his stomach often echoed jealous growls as I sat at the table to eat lunch with the children we were caring for. God ultimately honored Mark's diligence and sacrifice.

After gaining approval from our denomination, we began construction of a high-rise hospital in the heart of the city. Obtaining the property alone was a miracle. The land was a nineteenth century British cemetery, which in itself had dissuaded superstitious Hindus and Muslims from submitting a bid for the acreage.

Even after the land was acquired, we faced a perplexing situation. Squatters had built makeshift homes in the corner of the property, and we knew it would be frowned upon if we asked the authorities to remove them from their hovels. We were at somewhat of an impasse, unsure exactly how God would have us deport the squatters from His estate.

One afternoon, a fire broke out on the property. The squatters fled to escape the flames and never returned. Within days, the digging of the foundation began.

But like a nightmarish brand of deja vu, the digging stopped. Muddied water seeped into the hole and formed what looked like an unfiltered swimming pool.

Mark recognized this as a last-ditch effort by the enemy to halt the erection of this monument to God. We summoned numerous employees together for a time of intercession around the hole. Mark led us in prayer, asking God to perform another miracle. Mark appeared undaunted by the standstill, yet I had to wonder if, deep within, he feared his labors had been in vain.

To myself, I prayed, "God, please help us. Mark has worked so hard, and we've gotten so close to seeing this hospital built. Please don't let this discourage him. Give him the faith he needs to see Your work carried on."

Before the week was through, the seepage stopped and building commenced. But the enemy wasn't through with his attacks—and the next blow came from a totally different direction. We discovered that a man was trying to splinter one of our seven non-English speaking congregations from the church. I had sensed some disloyalties emerging and had reported this to Mark.

In prayer one morning God revealed to Mark where a list of dissidents was being kept. With that list in hand, Mark approached members of the faction and defused a split before it started. Still the enemy wasn't finished.

We had started the hospital with a fraction of the funding necessary. To Mark that was faith; for others, including myself, it was illogical. But I had seen God perform too many miracles to doubt Mark's leadership.

Our accountant came to me with lines under his eyes. I could sense by the tone of his voice that he had lost sleep the night before worrying about our financial predicament.

He said, "The feeding program is broke. We are in trouble, Mrs. Buntain. We don't have enough money to keep it going. Should I tell Pastor Buntain?"

I thought for a moment before responding. In times past I had withheld such information from my husband until I had calculated a solution I could offer as a suggestion. But this was a major crisis, and I knew he had to be informed. Besides, this time I didn't have a solution to recommend.

Mark responded to the crisis in typical fashion. Together with our accountant, we joined hands and prayed that God would provide the desperately needed funds.

A few days passed, and our food lines were on the verge of closing when a substantial check arrived in the mail. I wanted to dance all over the office. The accountant was also amazed and grateful. Whenever our funds were low in the years that followed, he always reminded us of this incident. Mark, of course, was also thankful, but he reacted without astonishment.

Sometimes I was awed by my husband's faith; other times it was perturbing because I felt like I had to worry for the two of us. We were in the process of building a hospital without any certainty the incoming contributions would underwrite the project. It was hard to believe we were bankrolling the working contractors and engineers and the tens of barefooted coolies hauling wood and bags of cement on their pull carts—let alone a feeding program and a school.

"Mark," I exclaimed, "how are we going to pay for all this?"

"Don't worry, God will take care of it."

I gave him a smirk of consternation.

"He's going to supply all we need. Don't worry," Mark replied confidently.

I said, "Worrying about money is my job, remember?"

Mark *had* heard from God. Each month, as he predicted, the offerings exceeded our expenses. Interested parties and congregations around the world provided the finest medical machinery and helped to fund what would become one of the most respected hospitals in India.

In March, 1977, we dedicated the hospital and research center. The complex that had gnawed at Mark for many years was now a reality. It had happened in God's timing.

# 34
# *No Room for Doubt*

As I dashed into my office to accept the phone call from Uncle Lionel, fear rushed through me, causing my hands to tremble. I knew he didn't call at this hour unless it was an emergency.

He said, "Your mother is seriously ill. They think it was a reaction to the cortisone she was taking for her arthritis. I don't know if she's going to make it. You need to come as soon as you can. She's slipped into a coma."

Since arriving in Calcutta, I had become far too familiar with death—almost numb. I had witnessed the sordid spectacle of dying patients and corpse-like beggars and had come to the place where it seldom made me teary-eyed. Yet Mother's condition had wrenched my emotions, and I was reminded just how awful death can be. I wept inwardly as I listened to Uncle Lionel's trembling voice.

When I arrived at the door of Mother's hospital room three days later, I was imagining her as she was at my wedding: a rare combination of beauty and strength. But the woman I saw under the white sheet had no resemblance to the woman in my daydreams. Her beautiful face had become swollen and unsightly.

Bonnie had flown to Vancouver and was standing beside me when I leaned over the bed and said, "Mother," hoping my voice would revive her.

Nothing but her lungs moved. Her heavy breathing was all that could be heard. The hush was haunting.

The room quaked as Beulah jarred the door. We embraced, each hating that this reunion had been initiated by Mother's deathly condition. Beulah had done well in real estate, just as I knew she would, and she and Bob had a lovely family. But for a brief moment it was as if we were children again, wanting to pounce on Mother's bed to wake her so she could fix us our Saturday morning breakfast.

By the time I arrived at the hospital, the doctor had already admitted to Uncle Lionel it was only a matter of time before she passed on. Gangrene had attacked her ulcerated leg, and they had been forced to amputate it while my plane was en route. The hospital had kept Mother alive by an artificial support system until I arrived.

Two days later she passed into eternity. I felt cheated—not having the chance to speak to her. Before leaving the hospital, I re-entered Mother's room for one last glance at the face I hoped I could forget. The broad shouldered, attractive woman was no more, but the inscription she had made on my life was eternal.

Uncle Lionel found it especially difficult to deal with Mother's death. He had somehow defied the aging process. His hair was gray, but his physique would have made a man in his thirties proud. But inside I could see his spirit crumbling.

After we buried Mother beside my father, Uncle Lionel returned to Calcutta with me. But Mother's illness had taken its toll on him. Many nights he had surrendered his sleep to keep one eye guarding his dear sister. Not long after he came to stay with us, Uncle Lionel had to be hospitalized for exhaustion.

I admired Uncle Lionel as one who had sacrificed his own wants to become the caretaker of others. He stayed with us six months, and during that period he often reminisced about my mother and grandmother, relaying story after story of their grandeur. The anecdotes elicited tears and laughter.

I couldn't help but wonder aloud on occasion—especially when I was alone and feeling forgotten—why Mother had to die before I had a chance to express the depth of my love for her. She died shortly before experiencing the birth of her great grandson and my first grandson, James Mark. I couldn't understand why God could not have delayed her passing. But after all Mark and I had experienced, there was no room for doubting the Lord's sovereignty and wisdom.

It would be misleading to suggest I have never doubted God's sovereignty or wondered if He would come to our rescue. In 1981, when our hospital workers went on strike, I certainly feared for my life.

On Christmas day, Mark left our flat—against my warnings—to open the feeding program on the hospital grounds. He returned several hours later, having been jostled around by a few hostile workers. His shirt was torn, his glasses were broken, and his hair was a tangled mess.

As time wore on, the instigators of the strike began leading protest marches against us and the hospital. Every day they surrounded our house and beat on the gate downstairs. More than fifty employees chanted outside our window and wrote profanities on the walls of our building. We were understandably afraid to exit the front door of our apartment complex.

Mark had no choice but to close the hospital until the dispute was resolved. Labor leaders had promised the workers they would get higher wages if they went on strike. The majority of employees were satisfied with their wage, yet they willingly followed the boisterous few leading the revolt.

As the strike reached its ninth month, the mob had diminished to a handful. The case went to court, and the judge ordered the workers back to work at their previous wage. They gladly returned to their jobs and halted their participation in the rallies.

To survive in Calcutta—especially as a Caucasian woman—I had to develop a backbone of sorts. Actually, I had to learn to look courageous even though on the inside I might be trembling.

"Auntie Buntain, come quickly! A man is threatening to take all our cans," Annie, our feeding program director, yelled into the phone. Metal cans were a valuable commodity in Calcutta.

Jumping in the rear seat of my car, I shouted my destination to a church-employed driver. Within minutes I was at the Royd Street property, running like an olympian to intercept the intruder in a narrow passageway. He came to a sliding stop. His shoulder length hair was damp from perspiration, and an unbuttoned shirt revealed his muscular chest. I recognized the young man. He had a reputation on Royd Street as a black marketeer. Rumors of his fighting ability and extortion schemes had circulated among the church people. In fact, he had made similar attempts to take church property before.

I said sharply, "If you've hurt Annie, you're going to have to deal with me, too. What is it you want?"

As he strode closer, I noticed a menacing knife wedged between his belly button and pants. He grinned as if I would be his next victim.

"What is it you want?" I snarled.

"Cans, your old cans."

"They've already been sold. They belong to someone else."

The passageway was barely large enough for two children to squeeze through. He took another step, but I stood still.

He knew he would have to go through me if he wanted to leave the compound.

I pointed my finger at his chest and scolded, "How dare you threaten Annie."

He snorted, inhaled deeply, then sighed as if surrendering.

"Come with me," I said, tugging on his arm. I yelled at him all the way to my office.

To my astonishment, once inside, he apologized like a felon seeking probation. The young man ducked his chin and eyes and said, "I'm sorry."

I was surprised and somewhat skeptical of his change of heart. I just stared into his scarred face, seeking a glimmer of sincerity.

"I'm sorry," he repeated.

I dismissed him without calling the police. Before the day was through, news of the confrontation had spread throughout the community, and a teenage boy had compared me to his hero, Muhammad Ali.

On another occasion my proclivity for peacekeeping nearly proved fatal. Two boys were fighting with blades on the church premises. Without thinking, I ran into the middle of their skirmish and suddenly realized their weapons were only inches from my flesh.

"Get out of the way, *Auntie* Buntain, or you're going to get hurt," the taller boy sneered.

Both boys were known drug users, so I didn't take anything for granted. He might truly carry out his threat.

I shouted, "Stop it! Do you hear me? Stop it!"

Even the bystanders who had formed a ring around the fighters were stung by my commanding tone.

"Put those away. Do it, now!"

One, followed by the other, met my demand, and the eager mob dispersed.

It was reminiscent of the time a young man pounded his fist on my desk, then raised a machete in defiance to the suspension of his brother from our boys' home. I calmly, although unadvisedly, removed the sword from his hand, and the quarrel was settled without incident.

One dispute led to an appearance in court. A former employee, who claimed we had fired him unduly and had kept him from locating other employment, had filed a grievance with the local authorities.

I entered the courtroom with my knuckles sweating profusely. Embers of disgust were fueled inside me as I spotted the plaintiff who was trying to extort a financial settlement.

The judge, robed in his black gown, kept his eyes glued to the bench when he asked me to stand in the witness box.

"Are you Huldah Buntain?"

"Yes, your Honor," I answered.

"Do you know this man? Did you hire him?" he asked, pointing his finger at the former employee.

"Yes."

"Are the accusations he has made against you true?"

"No, your Honor. He wasn't doing his work. He was lazy, and we can't afford to pay people to sit around. Every extra cent is used to treat patients and provide our school children with everything they need."

The judge, after writing some notes on a pad, lifted his head. He glanced at the plaintiff then looked over my shoulder—never into my eyes. "I will give you the court's decision next week," he said.

When I returned to the courtroom a week later, the judge was rubbing his gray sideburns while studying a sheaf of papers. The room was shrouded with silence as he prepared to divulge his decision. My pounding heart was the only sound I could hear.

Without explanation and without emotion, the judge announced, "Case dismissed."

I wanted to thank the magistrate for not falling for the man's scheme, but he left the courtroom immediately.

The former employee fled from the courtroom in a huff, as if angels of mercy were clapping their wings so loudly it was excruciating to his deceitful ears. To my ears, it was like a flawless symphonic rendition.

# 35
## Pressing On

With the success of *The Compassionate Touch,* a book based on the ministry in Calcutta, Mark received international exposure. He began receiving invitations to appear on radio and television programs and to speak in the largest churches around the world. Almost overnight, his name had become a household word among evangelicals. As a result, raising funds became an easier task, and, in a few short years, our hospital, schools, boys' home, and other programs were having a greater influence on the city. Nearly two thousand were attending the Sunday morning services in our eight congregations, more than twenty thousand were being fed daily, and thousands were enrolled in our seventeen schools and being treated in our hospital.

Suddenly, accolades and recognition adorned us like a newly crowned king and queen. No longer were we an obscure missionary team, praying religious leaders would accept our phone calls or respond to our letters.

Despite his "celebrity status," Mark's vision for Calcutta never changed. He didn't change. Attempts to lure him from India with lucrative offers never seemed to tempt him. His eyes were fixed on one goal—reaching the people of this forsaken land for Christ through meeting their physical and educational needs.

Mark's vision drove him to travel thousands of miles each year preaching the gospel and raising funds for the hospital and school. On some nights he literally collapsed into his hotel bed after preaching a fervent message. He often deprived himself of sleep to intercede for a need brought to his attention. While traveling, Mark frequently sacrificed meals to pray and read his Bible alone.

On one such tour, a music group from our church accompanied Mark to the States. They were ministering in Texas, and I was in Missouri visiting Bonnie when I received a phone call from a member of the group. He said, "Mark is having trouble with his leg, and he's flying to the hospital at Oral Roberts University to see an orthopedic surgeon." The doctor, Al Holderness, was a member of the Calcutta Mission of Mercy Board of Directors, so I knew Mark would receive excellent care. It was obvious to me, however, that Mark had to be experiencing serious discomfort for him to leave the tour to fly to ORU.

The next afternoon, Dr. Holderness called to inform me that Mark was scheduled for surgery the following morning for a ruptured disc. A thousand blurred thoughts flashed through my mind that day.

The traveling, toting heavy luggage, and lifting all his children in Calcutta had rendered him helpless—unable to walk or pivot without pain. I wanted to be there to ease the suffering, to utter comforting words, but instead I had to take Mark's place that night in the pulpit of Central Assembly in Springfield, Missouri.

Following the Friday night service, I drove to Tulsa and arrived just in time to see him waking from the anesthesia. Before speaking, his eyes repeatedly sealed and unsealed. Because he was stumbling over his words and inferring that he was in Calcutta, I surmised he was having an adverse reaction to the medication.

"Mark, you're in Tulsa—the United States," I said, annunciating each syllable.

He moaned and then dozed off.

I leaned back in my chair in his hospital room and talked to God. "Thank You, Father, for giving us a successful surgery. But what reason could You have for allowing this to happen?"

I wasn't visited by an angel that day, nor did I hear an audible voice, but I was assured in my heart that God was watching over us—even in the midst of my doubts and temporary tantrums.

Mark would recover, albeit a slow process to be sure. Dr. Holderness had advised Mark to limit his preaching to thirty minutes. I wanted to say, "Bless you!" to the doctor when I heard his suggestion because I thought my husband preached too long anyway.

When Mark eventually returned to the pulpit months later, he was free of pain as long as he was preaching. As a result, my husband retained his passion for lengthy messages. When he returned to our flat afterwards, however, he would often toss and turn in agony. I didn't enjoy being a nag; I just hated to see him suffer when my warnings went unheeded. Before services I advised, "Don't preach long tonight." During services I twirled my watch from the audience, hoping he would see me. After services I chided, "It serves you right, young man."

Mark often responded, "You sound like a broken record." We meant nothing derogatory by our verbal and non-verbal exchanges. In fact, if I hadn't expressed concern, I think he would have been disappointed.

Mark seldom complained. If someone asked how he was feeling, he would say, "Pressing on." I was more transparent, occasionally verbalizing my weariness and my longing to see my family. Responding to my murmuring, Mark would say in jest, "Here lies Huldah Buntain who gave her life for the souls of India; here lies a martyr." Every time he uttered that parody, I was reminded of just how fortunate we were. God had truly given our family more than we could ever acknowledge.

Four months after Mark's surgery, I found myself asking God the "why" questions all over again. I was in the States when I received word that Mark had injured his back again and required another operation.

I had left him in Calcutta just three weeks earlier, and he seemed to be moving freely without pain. The truth is, with Mark one could never be sure what, if any, pain he was experiencing. To him, complaining was synonymous with giving the enemy praise.

Mark was the last passenger off the plane in St. Louis. I gasped as I witnessed the attendant pushing him in a wheelchair like an invalid. I had not prepared myself for the severity of his condition.

Mark underwent corrective surgery a few days later, and we listened to the doctor repeat his recuperative instructions. I cringed at the thought of reliving Mark's period of recovery. While recuperating, he was always like a caged animal being tormented by a slab of raw meat suspended just beyond its reach. Returning to help the throbbing needs of Calcutta's poor and spiritually destitute was the prize he yearned for, yet this time his frail spine made a hasty return impossible.

# 36
# *Gone But Not Forgotten*

"Huldah, Ed's gone," my sister-in-law Alice announced on the other end of the telephone.

I looked at the alarm clock—2:30 a.m.

"What do you mean he's 'gone'?" I asked; "gone where?"

"No, he's dead," she cried.

"What are you saying?" I stammered.

Alice responded with noises I never knew she could make. From my bed in Missouri, two thousand miles from Tacoma, I listened to her cry, unable to ease her mourning. At least two minutes passed before she could relay what had happened.

Ed and Alice had eaten dinner with their daughter, Suzanne, and her husband. Afterwards, Ed went to lie down for a nap. Moments later, the family heard a loud thump upstairs. They rushed in to find Ed lying on the bedroom floor. The paramedics temporarily revived him but lost the pulse in the ambulance. Ed had died of a massive heart attack.

Hours after hearing the details from Alice, Bonnie, Maureen, and I caught a flight from Columbia, Missouri to Tacoma. Mark, who was holding meetings on the West

Coast, met us there. Fulton and Lorraine, who were pastoring in Tacoma, were already comforting Alice when we arrived.

There weren't many empty words shared during the many hours we spent with Alice over the next few days. Mostly, there were tears and hugs and memories of a jovial man who was synonymous with fun. Ed sometimes approached a complete stranger, usually an overweight woman, and would say, "Huldah! Aren't you Huldah Buntain?" Invariably, the woman set him straight, and he in turn apologized by saying, "I'm sorry, you look just like her."

In restaurants Ed drew the attention of the patrons by belting out a stanza of "Blessed Assurance" from our table. We tried to hide our faces while Maureen stared at him with her big eyes as if to say, "You're crazy!"

Ed had the ability to make Mark laugh like no one else could. Whenever Ed thought Mark was becoming too serious, he would raise a hand and shout "hoshiniai" to bring levity to the conversation. He loved to laugh and to make others laugh. His gift brightened many lives and brought comic relief to many situations.

Throughout the funeral, my arm was wrapped around Alice's shoulder. Wells of tears were spilling over onto our faces—even Mark's. I wanted to empathize with Alice and harbor some of her pain, but I couldn't imagine how difficult it would be to lose one's husband. With as many times as Mark had betrayed death, as strange as it may seem, I could never picture myself as a widow.

With her white handkerchief making a striking contrast against her black dress, Alice kept her head bowed throughout the ceremony. Her children did likewise, afraid to listen too intently to the eulogies. The speakers' words praised their father as if he were angelic. And, I had to admit, he was missing only a set of wings and a halo.

The trek to the burial site was like the Via Dolorosa, only I couldn't carry Alice's cross. As we stared at his casket beside the open grave, my memory was scalded by the corpse-like images of my parents and grandparents.

Then I thought of how Ed and Alice had visited us in Calcutta, and the four of us had tried to sing as a quartet again. The congregation roared with laughter that morning. But that pleasant memory could not overshadow the gruesome finality of this scene.

I turned to Mark, seeking his chest to cry on. As I put my ear to his heart, I could hear it pounding with determination. I basked in his arms and couldn't help but thank God *he* was alive.

# 37

## *An Angel of Mercy*

Flights back to Calcutta are fretful, lonely journeys, especially after spending too many days in North America with my family. It was never easy to leave my loved ones for a place like Calcutta. On this occasion it was especially difficult because Maureen would not be there to greet me; she had moved to America to live with Bonnie. I wasn't anxious to resume my hectic fourteen hour work days. I also dreaded the upcoming Saturdays. Because I didn't have a staff to manage or a cluttered desk to plunge into on weekends, I was left to conjure mental pictures of my girls and grandsons, wondering how they were spending their day and wishing I was there to enjoy it with them.

Knowing I would be coming back to the States and my family in eight months would make this particular return flight bearable, so I thought, as I boarded the plane in Columbia, Missouri for St. Louis. From St. Louis I would fly to Chicago to catch my international flight.

On our way to Chicago, uncooperative weather threatened to detour our plane to another airport.

"Ladies and gentlemen," the pilot announced over the intercom, "due to poor weather conditions we have just been re-routed to Minneapolis. I apologize for the delay. Representatives will be on hand there to assist you with connecting flights or overnight accommodations."

The word "assist" struck me funny, for the only assistance I wanted required a pilot and an airplane to get me to Calcutta where Mark was expecting me. We had been separated for too many weeks already, and I was growing too attached to my family and the comforts of the States.

After spending many hours in the air but landing nowhere because of heavy snowstorms and ice on runways, we deboarded about midnight where we had originated—blustery St. Louis. I didn't know what to do. The storm was growing fierce, and the airport was crowded. No jetliners were leaving the city, and I had already missed my flight in Chicago.

With mixed emotions I asked a porter to load my three large suitcases onto a cart and wheel them into the torrential winds bombarding the terminal. The blast of air nearly bowled us over. Taxis were blaring their horns viciously, nudging their way out of the chaos. Passengers were three rows deep raising their fists to summon a taxi. The porter set my bags down and walked back inside, marooning me in the fierce storm. My glasses were clouded by the breath of steam coming from my mouth. I pulled up my collar to shield my neck from the icy wind.

Fifteen minutes passed before passengers no longer outnumbered taxis. I waved to one driver across the island. "Taxi, taxi!"

The bearded driver poked his head out his window and yelled, "Bring your bags over here, lady. I can't come over there."

"They're too heavy," I responded using my cupped hands as a megaphone.

Throwing up his hands, he said, "I can't leave the cab. It's not permitted."

My heart sank to my stomach with despair. I whispered, "God, help me," as I tried to drag one of the huge suitcases across the sidewalk. Heavier snow was now falling, and the wind was whipping into my face. Suddenly, a large woman with bulging biceps appeared from nowhere.

She asked in the kindest voice imaginable, "Are you in distress, lady?"

"Am I ever."

"Do you want these over in that cab?"

"That would be wonderful."

Before I knew it, she had carried them across the island and lifted them into the trunk. As she started to gambol back to the terminal, I noticed she wasn't wearing a coat in subfreezing weather.

"Wait," I said, "let me pay you something for your trouble."

"No, no, I am just an angel of mercy tonight."

She disappeared inside, and I asked the driver, "Have you ever seen that woman before?"

"No, never. I thought she was with you."

"No, she wasn't," I said drifting back into my seat.

He added, "But I thought it was a little strange that she wasn't wearing a coat."

I cleaned my glasses and peered at the myriad of lights on the freeway. Out of all these people and all the needs they have, God chose to send me an angel of mercy to cross that island. "Lord, You really must love me," I whispered.

And from heaven I could almost see God leaning over his throne and saying, "That I do, my dear Huldah. That I do."

# ——38——
## *In His Hands*

Fallen leaves were everywhere the day we walked onto
the campus of the University of Missouri where Mark was
to receive an honorary doctorate. My son-in-law Jim was to
be awarded his second doctorate in the same ceremony. A
year earlier he had completed his medical doctorate.

The campus resembled an Ivy League school the way the
climbing vines hugged the sides of buildings and brick walls.
Typically, students were scurrying to classes with books
tucked under their arms. Some collegians were stretched out
on lawns; others were leaning against cement pillars. Just
being on a college campus made me feel young again.

When Mark marched to the podium to accept the framed
certificate, I felt like the wife of a medical student who had
just put her husband through years of training. The college
had taken two years to research our work in Calcutta; Mark
was the first non-graduate to receive such an award.

After receiving the citation, Mark said, "I have two to
thank for all that has been accomplished among the hurting of Calcutta. First, let me thank my wife, Huldah. Over
the years, she has been faithful to me and our ministry and
has worked many hours to make everything possible. This

great honor tonight must be shared with her. I imposed my vision upon her over thirty years ago, but she accepted that vision as her own and has given her life, so many others might live. I love her so very much."

"Foremost," Mark continued, "I must express my praise for my God who so loves all the world that He gave His only Son so that those in Calcutta and those here tonight might have hope. He so loves all the hurting, the diseased, and the deceived. He so longs to help the needy, and I'm grateful He has allowed my wife and me to be two of His hands extended to the people of India."

Throughout his speech, I grappled with feelings of guilt and gratification—all simultaneously. Guilt for the countless times I wanted us to return to the States to be with Bonnie and our family, and gratification for God's understanding and willingness to tolerate my feelings.

I was proud that night, grateful to be the wife of a man with such faith and commitment. All my evenings of self-pity seemed to fade in my memory as I evaluated all that had been accomplished for the kingdom of God through our marriage-partnership.

For years Mark had endured great back pain. Two operations and months of wearing bulky braces had not relieved the agony brought on by the rigorous schedule he kept. Doctors recommended that a plate, implanted in his back, would give his spine more stability and alleviate some of the pressure.

Mark had already agreed to return to the United States for the back surgery when it nearly became unnecessary. On a pleasant day in January, 1987, Mark came to the breakfast table feeling sick. His bleached face was terrifying. I led him back to bed and intended to call a doctor. As soon as he hit the mattress, he grabbed his chest and released an awful, deep grunt.

As I hunched into the ambulance twenty minutes later, I felt like the wife of a gladiator who had suffered a debilitating defeat. Mark's heart had always been so strong. I was in a state of shock.

As he laid in the hospital bed with tubes and wires running across his body, I thought of Ed's funeral and wondered if the Almighty would be greeting Mark next. I trembled by the minute at the thought of living without him. But each fear that rose like an insurmountable wall was met with a prayer from my lips. Mark had shown me the power of prayer—the key to overcoming fears that seek to devastate our faith.

"Lord, I need him. Please let him live. There's too much to be done still. Calcutta needs him."

Then, almost as if God had interrupted my thoughts, it occurred to me that this ministry was God's, and if He so desired, He could raise up someone else as His servant to the city of Calcutta. I realized this ministry was not dependent on the Buntains, that our sacrifice and ministry gave us no guarantees for a long life. We could be replaced if God chose. Our lives were in His hands. He was our Creator, our Sovereign Judge.

Only then, in the still hours of the morning, could I pray: "Thy will be done, Lord."

I awaited God's verdict. Hours passed. Then two Indian doctors walked toward me from a distant door. I peered into their faces, hoping for a hint that would prepare me for their diagnosis. No clue emanated from their stoic faces.

"Mrs. Buntain, your husband is resting comfortably, but he needs to go to the States for surgery as soon as he's physically able to make the trip." Without him saying it, I knew the doctor was referring to the more advanced technology in America.

I regretted the notion of Mark leaving, for I knew he would insist I stay behind to administer the church, school, and hospital.

The day of his departure for the United States, Mark asked me to come to his bedside. He wanted to talk to me alone.

He asked, "Do you know how serious my surgery is?"

"Yes, Jim told me."

"I want you to promise me two things."

I nodded as I squeezed his hand.

"If I don't survive the surgery, I want you to bring my body back to India to be buried."

Again I nodded, fighting back the tears.

He continued. "And I want you to promise me that you'll stay in Calcutta and carry on the mission."

"Mark," I assured, "you're not going to die. Hundreds of surgeries like yours are successful each year."

"I know, and I think God is going to bring me through, but I want you to promise me just in case something should happen. Will you?"

"I will," I vowed, though wanting to believe I would never have to fulfill my promise.

Jim met Mark's plane at the airport in Columbia and had him transported to the hospital. After tests were conducted, Bonnie telephoned me to confirm Mark would be undergoing open heart surgery in an hour.

I alerted members of the church and staff, and we gathered for an impromptu prayer meeting. Many tears were shed that morning.

The waiting was torturous. Knowing what Mark had made me promise before he left, I was worried that he had had a premonition of his death. I stared at the phone, begging it to ring with an update from Bonnie.

When she finally called, I surmised by her vibrant voice that the surgeons had declared the operation a success. How I had wanted to be there when Mark's eyes opened and the doctors conveyed the glowing report.

Not until June, 1987, would I see Mark face to face. God's grace sustained me during three months of separation from the man I loved. I vowed this time to stay by his side and put an end to this madness, but I knew deep inside nothing would change. He was married to both me and his work, and I wanted nothing more than for him to accomplish everything God had called him to do. Although our lifestyles—our chosen course—had filled me with moments of loneliness, never did I doubt his love or devotion, nor did I feel neglected.

# 39
## *I Love Calcutta*

Some months later, as I returned from a brief visit in the States with Jim, Bonnie, Maureen, and my three grandchildren, I found myself laid over in Bangkok for the night.

I released an exquisite sigh from the balcony of my hotel room. Bangkok had, uncharacteristically, become as tranquil as a Canadian lake at dawn. Tomorrow morning I would continue my journey home—to Calcutta—to the bustling office and the pressures of administrating a ministry on which thousands depended for their survival.

"Tomorrow," I preached to myself, "will come soon enough. Think about all God has given you, how He has taken care of you and Mark. Think about your family and all He has done to help the needy of Calcutta. Dwell on the light rather than the darkness."

Gratifying images of Mark, Bonnie, Maureen, Larissa, Jim, my grandchildren, Beulah, Alice, Uncle Lionel, the Mission of Mercy hospital, orphanages, schools, and feeding program swept through my mind. I knew I was one of the most fortunate women to ever live. God had taken an uncooperative teenager and sent her to a despairing place where she could make a difference.

Gazing into the stars, moments later, tears began seeping from my eyes as I thought of my woeful city. I wept for the distressed people. I wept for the diseased children. I wept because I loved Calcutta.

# 40
# *A Treasure in Heaven*

Months passed, and life was as rich and full as ever. In fact, Mark and I were making plans to purchase a new home in the States.

Bonnie had written that Jim had been selected to join a prestigious team of doctors conducting research on the artificial heart at the University of Utah Medical Center. Consequently, Jim, Bonnie, and the grandchildren began preparing to move to Salt Lake City.

To be near our loved ones when we were in the States, Mark and I decided to sell our modest home in Columbia, Missouri and move to Utah as well. We had purchased the house in Columbia only two years earlier. It was the first home we had ever owned, and it had become a place of refuge for us. More importantly, it had been a sanctuary where Mark could recover from his surgeries.

On Saturday, June 3, 1989, Mark and I were having lunch together in Calcutta—just before I was to leave for Salt Lake City to begin searching for a new home. Bonnie and Maureen would be there waiting for me. I said, "Mark, you don't have to go with me to the airport."

"I want to go," he said. "I want to see you off."

"It's too hot, and you need to stay off your feet," I reasoned. "Besides, you have a cold, and you'll have a long day tomorrow."

He ultimately agreed to stay put. We embraced, I exited, and he laid down to get some rest.

Ten minutes after I walked out of our flat, he became ill and collapsed onto the floor. His left leg had gone numb. By the time paramedics lifted him into an ambulance, Mark had lost consciousness. His left side was paralyzed, and his left eye had dilated.

People from the ministry tried unsuccessfully to reach me by phone at the Calcutta airport. As a result, I didn't receive word that Mark had suffered a cerebral hemorrhage until I reached my hotel room in Bangkok. I slumped down on my bed, wondering why God had allowed this to happen and why it had to happen just moments after I had left.

Regaining a semblance of composure, I went to the airport to get a flight back to Calcutta. Missionary Al Johnson and his wife, our long time friends, had met me in Bangkok and were helpful in securing the earliest return flight possible, which wouldn't be until the following afternoon.

The doctors who were operating on Mark Saturday evening had consulted with Jim in Columbia and, afterwards, felt the surgery had been a success. They kept me informed by periodically calling my hotel room in Bangkok. Hearing that Mark had feeling in both arms put my heart at ease. The doctors thought he would fully recover within a month or two. I went to sleep that night thanking God for saving Mark's life.

Sunday morning, I received a message to phone Ron Shaw, who had formerly served as Mark's senior associate.

"Hello, Ron," I said.

He quickly determined by the tone of my voice that I hadn't heard the latest news. He asked, "Have you heard from Calcutta?"

"Not this morning," I said.

"Huldah, Mark has gone to be with the Lord."

I gasped and cried as Ron tried to console me. The searing pain of that moment was unlike anything I had ever felt—a void beyond comparison.

When I landed back in Calcutta, many friends were waiting to offer their condolences. Loving, outstretched arms embraced me.

I was immediately taken to the funeral home to view Mark's body. Again I gasped, for I couldn't believe this lifeless form was the man I had embraced the day before. His head was bandaged, and his skin was white like cotton.

I was oblivious to my feelings during the next several hours, as if my nerves had been dulled. But pain jolted through my body when I walked into our bedroom and saw Mark's clothes hanging in our closet. He had gone away on ministry trips before but had always returned. He had been ill before but had always recovered. I was finally beginning to realize that Mark would never again walk up the stairs to our apartment.

The procession started at the funeral home and paused at the Royd Street property. There, government officials laid wreathes on Mark's casket, and others paid their respects. Shops along Royd Street pulled down their shades in honor of Mark—an act usually reserved for national dignitaries. The sidewalks were lined with mourning men, women, and children.

From Royd Street, with hundreds following the hearse, the procession continued on to Park Street, where an estimated twenty thousand were waiting for the funeral to commence. People stood on rooftops and peered out high-rise windows just to catch a glimpse of the ceremony. Religious leaders from Calcutta and around the world attended the ceremony and addressed the crowd.

Thousands passed by Mark's casket, many wailing with tears, others stopping to bend to one knee. Then, with the government's permission, Mark's casket was lowered into the foundation of the new sanctuary that was under construction.

The following Sunday morning, our congregations came together for a combined service. It was announced that the board had appointed me as senior pastor and chairman. Instantly, the large gathering of smiling, weeping faces stood to its feet with applause.

At that moment, a myriad of thoughts flashed through my mind. Finally I had the opportunity to retire from Calcutta to be with my family and the comforts of a different world. But as the clapping continued, I found myself permeated with the same divine call that had driven Mark. I sensed my own ordination to continue the work among the people of the land I had grown to love. That's what Mark wanted; now I knew that's what God wanted as well.

As I listened to the gracious ovation, I had to believe that those in the congregation were not the only ones clapping. For I knew there was one in heaven leading a band of angels in cheers of his own and shouting, "Don't worry, Huldah. God has everything under control!"

# *Postscript*

Huldah is simply referred to as "Auntie Buntain" by the thousands who look to her for comfort and leadership in Calcutta.

On her birthday each year, she is the recipient of countless cards and flowers. When she goes to the market, she is mobbed for attention. When she visits patients in the hospital, she can't get from her car to the lobby without people clamoring for her assistance. And whenever her car approaches the boys' home, children crowd around her door, wanting to touch her hand and be granted one of her loving smiles.

It is common to see her at the altar leading children to Christ after a church service or using her lunch break to counsel young people in a motherly way. Her dinner table is always full of hungry youngsters from the school and church.

An incessant stream of needy individuals come to her for aid. Huldah admits that she sometimes feels like she's trying to put the Atlantic Ocean in a teacup, yet her compassion never wavers.

Huldah, by her own admission, is not a saint. She is, however, a hardworking pastor, administrator, and mother who has sacrificed her dreams and aspirations so she and her husband could come to the desperate city of Calcutta and proclaim God's hope.

In the past, her face wasn't recognized on airplanes or in shopping malls like her husband's was. And seldom was she interviewed on national television or radio. To her credit, she has never sought notoriety. Prior to Mark's passing, she was content to work behind the scenes without recognition. And perhaps therein lies the theme of Huldah Buntain's life: "Do not lay up for yourselves treasures on earth . . . but lay up for yourselves treasures in heaven" (Matthew 6:19,20). Assuredly, when she walks through the pearly gates, untold treasures and accolades will be waiting.